A-Z
PRAGUE
CULTURE
GUIDE

# ■ LEGEND OF THE MAP ■

1. PRAGUE CASTLE
2. BELVEDERE
3. GOLDEN LANE
4. NATIONAL GALLERY – STERNBERG PALACE
5. NEW WORLD (NOVÝ SVĚT)
6. STRAHOV MONASTERY
7. NERUDA STREET
8. PETŘÍN HILL
9. LITTLE QUARTER SQUARE – CHURCH OF ST NICHOLAS
10. CHURCH OF VICTORIOUS VIRGIN MARY – LITTLE JESUS
11. WALLENSTEIN PALACE AND GARDEN
12. CHARLES BRIDGE
13. SMETANA MUSEUM
14. THEATRE ON THE BALUSTRADE
15. CLEMENTINUM
16. OLD TOWN SQUARE – JAN HUS MONUMENT
17. UNGELT
18. THE NATIVE HOUSE OF FRANZ KAFKA
19. JAN PALACH SQUARE – RUDOLFINUM (CZECH PHILHARMONIC)
20. JEWISH QUARTER (GHETTO) AND OLD JEWISH CEMETERY
21. F. BÍLEK'S VILLA
22. HANAVSKÝ PAVILION AND PLACE OF STALIN'S MONUMENT
23. ST AGNES CONVENT
24. MUNICIPAL HOUSE
25. CAROLINUM
26. THE ESTATES THEATRE (STAVOVSKÉ DIVADLO)
27. WENCESLAS SQUARE
28. THEATRE BEHIND THE GATE
29. LATERNA MAGIKA
30. NATIONAL THEATRE
31. BABA
32. ADOLF LOOS' VILLA
33. STAR HUNTING LODGE
34. BERTRAMKA – MOZART'S MUSEUM
35. BARRANDOV
36. MÁNES
37. VYŠEHRAD
38. FAIR PALACE
39. EXHIBITION GROUNDS
40. TROJA CHATEAU

Jan Czech                    Jan Dvořák

# PRAGUE CULTURE GUIDE

Illustrated
by Michal Brix

Jan Czech – Jan Dvořák
A–Z PRAGUE CULTURE GUIDE
In cooperation with PhD. Jarmila Brožovská, Prof. František Dvořák
and PhD. Rostislav Švácha.
Drawings: Michal Brix (42) and Adolf Hoffmeister (1)
Photos : Jiří Jírů, ČTK Press Agency and archives of PRAGUE STAGE –
Jan Dvořák
Cover & Typo © Milan Pašek
Setting & Film: Šilar DTP
Printed by EKON Jihlava

ISBN: 80-901671-1-X

"Prague doesn't let go, this mother has claws.
One has to yield or on both sides burn it,
from Vyšehrad and Hradčany, only then it would be
possible to tear yourself free..."

**FRANZ KAFKA**

*Thank you for your confidence, expressed by keeping this book in hand, and for your feelings toward the most Prague has to offer– it's historical buildings, culture and art.*

*What is Prague? Look at a map of Europe and there it is, in the Czech lands at the heart of the continent, in its most sensitive region, there is Prague. From a historical viewpoint, Prague is among the oldest European towns and is presently one of the only Middle Age cities still preserved: from the tenth century Prague has retained its original town centre, located on the banks of Vltava river between Vyšehrad and the hill of Hradčany (Prague Castle).*

*From the earliest recorded history of the region, Prague has been celebrated for its size and industry: the early Arabic–Hebrew trader Ibrahim Ibn Jacob traveling through central Europe in 965–6 noted that Prague was the largest and busiest city, built of mortar and stone.*

*After the Velvet Revolution of 1989, Prague began anew its tradition of an international cross section of inhabitants which include tens million visitors and tourists, as well as unique communities such as the young enterprising Americans who number between twenty and thirty thousand. They follow on a long tradition of cultural distinctive communities, for example, the Vlašská quarter of Malá Strana which was once was home for a strong community of Italians who mostly served as the builders of Prague's Renaissance and Baroque architecture, and the tension produced between the Czech and German communities, headed up by a strong presence of Jews, resulted in an extremely enriched spiritual and cultural life as well as industrial and economic development of the city.*

In this way the rich treasures of the city were born and many of these gems are still preserved in Prague: Gothic, Baroque, Secese, and modern Functionalist architecture, not to mention its unique Cubists rarities– no other place in the world boasts Cubism comparable to that realized and preserved in Prague.

In reflection the famous Czech poet Jan Neruda said "what we find on a simple walk through Prague are real poems".

The beauty of its mystery and magnificence, its secrets and hidden wonders, attract us again and again to Prague. The theatre great George Tabori said "Prague has been a legend to me for many years, the magical place of my images. This, my Prague, is inhabited by many fascinating figures beginning with Golem and Schweik... and ending with Franz Kafka".

This lifestyle, a harmony of the city's mystery and its magical art of famous composers, musicians, poets, painters, sculptors, and architects, many who continue to work here, makes Prague a magnet to the young and creatice–minded people who come from across oceans and from around the world, drawn to Prague as their grandfathers were drawn to Paris after World War I.

And it should be mentioned too that the informal and unconventional guide you hold in your hands was not written by cosmopolitan travel experts, who wrote yesterday about Singapore and who will write about Rio de Janeiro tomorrow, but by top domestic experts in love with Prague, whose life study has been Prague. These venerable and respected specialists know their topic from top to bottom and are therefore able to meaningfully characterize and describe the phenomena. Thus this book is not a step–by–step guide or an impersonal list of place–names, it is an informatorium of the true Prague's cultural minimum, without which your steps through town may lack a deeper and more valuable understanding: it is a first wholesome orientation.

*Since 1991, Prince Charles of Wales, the heir to the British throne, has visited Prague three times. The Prince believes the centre of the old town should be an unique architectonic reservation. He organized a reception in London's St. James Palace to help fund the restoration of Prague's old buildings (Prague's Historical Fund). The photograph shows the Prince on a walk through Old Town Square.*

*The book is alphabetized from A–Z and includes important persons, phenomena, architectural epochs, and famous historical monuments, buildings and curiosities; topics within sections expanded upon in their own sections are highlighted in bold print; the last portion of the book contains a complete and updated compilation of cultural institutions and services for visitors to Prague.*

*There is nothing left but to wish you all the best in your reading, in expanding your interest and knowledge of one of the most beautiful cities in the world.*

JAN DVOŘÁK – Editor

# ■ ST. AGNES – ANEŽKA PŘEMYSLOVNA ■

St. Agnes is an important religious figure in the Czech history. She was born in 1211, the daughter of Czech King Přemysl I and his wife Konstancie Uherská, sister of King

*Convent of St Agnes*
*(founded in 1233)*

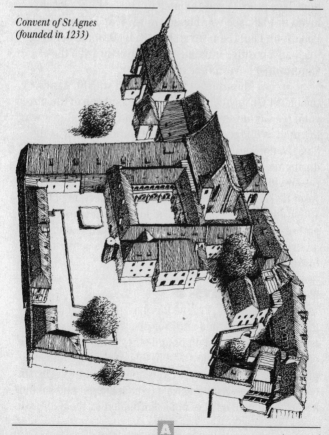

Václav I. She worked to stabilize her father's state, promoted education, and founded the men's college later consecrated as the Church of the Knights of the Cross.

Inspired by the example of St. Francis of Assisi, she established the "Na Františku" monastery in Prague for the poor, the sick and crippled, and for wayfarers. This led to the establishment of similiar charities in Bohemia focusing on social care. St. Agnes died on March 2, 1282, and, although she was buried at the monastery, the floods of 1322-3 resulted in the removal and ultimate disappearance of her remains. This, in part, delayed her canonization. This process was initiated by Queen Eliška Přemyslovna in 1328, she was blessed in 1874, and canonized by Pope John Paul II on November 12, 1989. Some believe this had a positive influence in the overthrow of the **Communist** government a week later.

St. Agnes Monastery, closely aligned with St. Agnes, is the oldest **Gothic** complex in Prague and one of the most valuable Gothic structures in Bohemia. Adjacent to it was the men's college of the Minorits Church, as well as the St. Salvador and St. František churches. It was destroyed during the Hussite wars and rebuilt, then damaged by fires and invasions. Finally it was abandoned by Emperor Josef II. Today the **National Gallery's** collection of Czech 19th Century Art is exhibited at the monastery as well as part of the Art and Industry Museum collection and part of an exhibitiion dedicated to the monastery's construction history.

## ■ ANTIKVARIATS ■

As a cultural centre, Prague has played a crucial role in the book business, and antikvariats, which sell used and antique books, prints, maps and other printed items, have played an important part within this role, located near publishing houses, literary **cafes**, and bookstores. The state-owned chain of antikvariats (which bought and sold in accordance with a list of books forbidden by the State) was discontinued after 1989. The stores rapidly came under ownership of expert antique booksellers who adjusted the ridiculously low state prices to match the value, according to West European standards. Today, antikvariats contain a good selection of valuable copies, rare first prints, bibliotheca, graphics and engravings.

Some of the best antikvariats include: Antikvariát Karla Křenka at No. 31 Celetná (also graphics and drawings), Antikvariát Karlův most (No. 2 Karlova Street), Antikvariát Můstek (No. 13 Ul. 28. října), the Jewish–Hebrew antikvariat at No. 7 Široká, in Old Town (Jewish quarter). The book specialist Václav Prošek has periodic auctions at his antikvariat, and his office is located at No. 42 Podolská, Praha 4–Podolí.

## ■ GUILLAUME APOLLINAIRE ■

Guillaume Apollinaire (1880–1918) is considered as one of the greatest poets of his era. Of Polish ancestry, the French poet was influential in modern art movements, particularly **Cubism** and **Surrealism**.

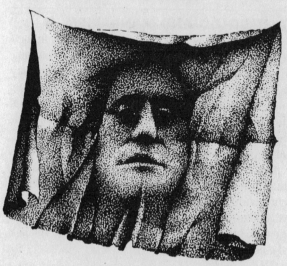

The author of *"Alcools"* and *"Calligrams"* visited Prague in early March 1902. The experiences gained during his short visit can be traced in a few of his poems. For example, he visited the restaurant U Rozvařilů across from the department store Bílá labuť, and from *"Prague's Walker"* we hear about the "pubs, where the Czech songs resound over paprika gulash, baked potato and cucumber, poppy seed rolls and bitter pilsen beer." From Apollinaire's notes, the French expert Marcel Decaudin, believes he visited the Jewish City Hall (Židovská radnice) and noticed the clock hands moving backwards, the Charles Bridge (Karlův most) where he admired the statues and the Vltava River, and the **Prague Castle**. In his famous poetry collection *"Zone"* he mentions being shown a semi–precious stone in the St. Vanc Chapel which "contains an image some believe is a portrait of Napoleon, but it is me!"

Thanks to this collection, Prague was further immortalized in the worlds' poetry. Apollinaire greatly influenced modern Czech art and artists, particularly the poets V. Nezval and **J. Seifert**, and art theoretician **K. Teige**.

## ■ ARCIMBOLDO AND MANNERISM ■

Mannerism is a style of art which emerged in Italy in the second half of the 16th century, transitional between the **Renaissance** and **Baroque** periods. Its earliest origins are found in the works of Michelangelo and Raphael in Rome. The most important centres of Mannerism were Mantova, (Giulio Romano) Italy, and later Fontainebleau in central France. Mannerism was a response to the simple Renaissance patterns of the masters. It was an intellectual movement which attempted to achieve certain effects to introduce shape and light. It required an increased sensual participation and creative imagination which verged on absurdism and aesthetic information. The climax and decline of Mannerism in Prague occurred around 1600, with the court of **Rudolph II**.

The remarkable art of Giuseppe Arcimboldo (1527–1593) was created at this time in Prague. He became famous for his paintings depicting human faces and using various objects as absurd metaphors to characterize topical themes. The paintings reflect an eccentric conjunction of science and magic, philosophy and mysticism. Arcimboldo began his career with window decorations for the Milan Cathedral and decorations for ceremonial occasions in Milan. It was his success in this area which resulted in his invitation to the Kaiser's Court in Vienna; however, his talent was only fully realised later, under Rudolph II who invited him to Prague. There Arcimboldo created his most remarkable works for Rudolph's collection. These works, created during a sixteen year stay in Prague, were later moved abroad. The Allegories of Summer and Winter from the Four Seasons cycle, as well as the two compositions Water and Fire from the Elements cycle, are exhibited in Vienna. Other works are in the Louvre and some collections are in Sweden. Only a few paintings, including a self–portrait and studies of Rudolph II as Czech King and Roman Emperor, remain in storage at Prague's **National Gallery**.

## ■ ART DECO ■

Interest in Art Deco has increased concurrently with postmodern art in general. The designation of this 1920's style was coined at the Exposition Internationale des Arts Décoratifs in Paris in 1925. The stylistic idea stemming from the simplistic vitality of popular art manifested by bold, streamlined and rectilinear forms, using modern materials, was defined first by architect Le Corbusier. In architecture, Art Deco found remarkable application in New York (for example, the Chrysler Building constructed in 1928 by William van Alen, who roofed it with an intricate headpiece of stainless steel). Art Deco tendencies provided big opportunities for the decorative arts, particularly in glass and jewelry.

Prague's Art Deco assumed special features through national decorative elements and late **Cubism**, or so–called Rondocubism. The architect Pavel Janák built (1922–4) the impressive Adria–Riunione Adriatica Palace at the corner of Národní třída and Jungmannova Street, and the Directorate of the Škoda Works at No. 29 Jungmannova Street. The Legio–bank building at No. 24 Na Poříčí, was built by Josef Gočár, and ornamented with sculptures by **O. Gutfreund**. Other noted Czech decorative artists included Jaroslav Horejc (glass work), František Kysela (book graphics, interior design and textile wall hangings) and Jaroslav Benda, an original designer of decorative calligraphy and postal stamps of the early 1920's. Early Art Deco interior designs include: the beautiful ceramic tiles of the cafe in the former Imperial Hotel at the corner of Na Poříčí and Zlatnická Street (designed by Josef Drahoňovský): other unique interiors are preserved at the Industrial Art school in Žižkov (Žižkovo náměstí, Praha 3), including the principal's office furniture and decorative windows by František Kysela, which were displayed at the famous Paris exposition in 1925; in the building at Mariánské náměstí, Praha 1, housing the main Municipal Library, the rooms of the Prague mayor, richly ornamented and preserved as a whole, and works of the architect František Roith from 1928 (only the library and the unique **puppet theatre** is accessible to the public through the side street entrance); and finally, there is a rare Art Deco newsstand from the 1920's, on Bolzanova Street at the end of the park in front of the Wilson train station (Hlavní nádraží).

## ■ ART NOUVEAU (SECESE) ■

Secese is a style from the time of the 1900's, its Czech name is taken from the Latin Secessere which means to go apart, and it represents a revolt of artists at the end of the last century against academical art and backward art schools. These artists felt a particular need for uniting artistic creation with normal life especially through architecture. The strongest movement in Munich and Berlin was called Jugendstil and in Vienna as Secessionstil, led by Gustav Klimt. In France it was called Art Nouveau and in London, Modern Style. The first Secese revolt was in Munich (1892) and is documented in the artists' magazine *Jugend*.

In 1898, Prague's Secese movement was united with the **Mánes** art group which included architect Jan Kotěra, sculptors Jan Štursa, Ladislav Šaloun, Stanislav Sucharda, and painters Jan Preisler, Max Švabinský, Vladimír Županský. Other Czech secese artists include: the painters

*Hanavský Pavilion (1891)*

**Alphonse Mucha** and František Kupka, who both lived in Paris, and also graphic artist Vojtěch Preissig, who lived from 1910 to 1930 in the USA. Examples of world famous Czech Secese include the **Obecní dům** building designed by Antonín Balšánek and Osvald Polívka, assisted by Prague artists Jan Preisler and Alphonse Mucha.

Another important figure in Secese art history is the architect Josef Fanta, the designer of Wilson Station and the House of Choir Hlahol (on Masaryk's Promenade adjacent to Mánes). The beautiful Secese buildings on **Wenceslas Square** include the Hotel Europa and Peterkův dům (No. 777), on Vodičkova the U Nováků House (No. 699), on Národní Street U Topičů House (No. 1010), and the nearby former State Insurance office at No. 1011, the Hotel Paříž behind Obecní dům, the former Chamber Theatre (the Hotel Central) at No. 1001 Hybernská Street, the Vinohrady Theatre, the Hanavský Pavilion at the Letná Orchards, and the Palace of Industry at Výstaviště (Exhibition Grounds). Monumental statues in the Secese–style include the **F. Palacký** Memorial in Prague 2 near Palackého Bridge and the **Jan Hus** statue in the Old Town Square.

# ■ THE BABA COMMUNITY ■

The huge success of the architectural exhibition "Die Wohnung" in Stuttgart, in 1927, which expressed the manifestos of the leading avant–garde architects concerning functionalist–style family homes, provided impetus for a series of similar expos across Europe, which, in central Europe included Brno (1928), Wroclaw–Breslau (1929), Vienna (1931), and Budapest (1931). In 1932 a collection of functionalist homes were constructed on a hilltop called Baba in Prague 6–Dejvice for an exhibition by the Czech Werkbund–Union of Czechoslovak Industries and Design. The blueprints for this unique development were developed by the group's long–time chairman, Pavel Janák (1882–1956).

The construction was not financed by the city or by the Werkbund group as were previous exhibits, but by the future owners themselves. The custom homes suited the lifestyle of those who commissioned them, and though not many were built, the ones that were, are very well

*The Baba Community (1932–1940)*

maintained and preserved. The majority of the community is located on Nad Paťankou, Jarní Street, Matějská Street, and Průhledová, and consists of 39 functionalist buildings built between 1932 and 1940. The most notable were designed by E. Linhart and A. Heythum (No. 1710 Na Ostrohu Street), Ladislav Žák (No. 1793 Na Ostrohu Street, No. 1782 Na Babě), Hana Kučerová–Záveská (No. 1781 Na Babě), František Kerhart (No. 1789 Nad Paťankou), Pavel Janák (No. 1795 Nad Paťankou), and Mart Stam, a well known left–oriented Dutch avant–gardist (No. 1779 Na Babě).

## ■ BAROQUE ■

Baroque represents an artistic style which was popular in Europe from the early 17th century to the mid 18th century, when it was replaced by **Rococo** style. It features a conjunction of church and palacial architecture. The Baroque cultural centre, and cradle of its creative force, was Rome, which had absorbed many of the spiritual and artistic personalities of the day. Anti–reformation forces in Prague concentrated significant personages from central Europe, especially Italy and Germany. The great Austrian architect Fischer von Erlach built one of the most important Baroque works in Prague, the Clam–Gallas Palace (No. 20 Husova Street). The palace was commissioned by the Viceroy of Naples, Count Jan Václav Gallas. Plans for the Prague Church of the Theatines were drawn up by the great Baroque designer Guarino Guarini but it was not built. Another great Roman Baroque architect, Carlo Fontana, designed Martinický Palace at the **Prague Castle** (No. 181 Loretánská Street), which was built in 1701–2 for Jiří Adam of Martinic, another Viceroy of Naples. Unfortunately it has served as a military hospital since 1837.
A deeper domestic rooting of the Baroque is attributed to the Italian artist Carlo Lurago, whose name is synonymous with the founding of the largest educational centre in central Europe, **The Clementinum**, situated between

the entrance of Karlův most (Charles Bridge), Karlova Street, and Mariánské náměstí.

Some of the fine Baroque architecture in Prague represents the work of domestic artists such as Kilián Ignác Dienzenhofer (1689–1751) and Giovanni Santini (1677–1723). Dienzenhofer's most renowned work is the Church of St. Nicholas in Malá Strana (Little Quarter), with the front facade created by his father Christoph. Dienzenhofer also designed a second St. Nicholas Church, this one located on Staroměstské náměstí (Old Town Square), and Kinský Palace, facing the church, houses the graphics collection of the **National Gallery**. Dienzenhofer's work also includes the facade at the famous Loretto at Prague Castle. Despite his Italian name, Giovanni Santini was a third generation Praguer. His work includes: Morzin Palace on Nerudova Street (the present Romanian Embassy), which is ornamented with a sculpture by Brokof; Schönborn Palace in Malá Strana (site of the United States Embassy); and Sternberg Palace at the Prague Castle, housing the National Gallery collection of ancient and modern masters.

Exceptional Baroque sculpture adorns the famous Charles Bridge (Karlův most), most notable of these are the statues of Ferdinand Maxmilian Brokof and Matthew Bernard Braun. Prague's hometown painter Karel Škréta was influenced by the international Baroque, his masterpiece decorates the main altar of the Church of the Virgin Mary in Front of the Týn Cathedral at Staroměstské náměstí.

*Clam–Gallas Palace
(1713–19)*

He was admitted to the Prague painters guild on the basis of this work. Other famous Prague Baroque painters include Petr Brandl and Václav Vavřinec Reiner, who specialized in frescos created for cathedrals. Brandl's work decorates St. Vitus Cathedral at Prague Castle, St. James Church in the Old Town, and St. Joseph's Church in the Little Quarter, which include early works before 1700. Reiner's most famous fresco is *"The Last Judgement"*, in the cupola of St. Francisco's Crossbearers Church on the Old Town side of the Charles Bridge. Additional precious Baroque areals are addressed separately under the following sections: <u>the Clementinum</u>, <u>Strahov Monastery</u>, <u>Troja Chateau</u> and <u>Wallenstein Palace</u>.

## ■ BARRANDOV ■

This district of Prague is named after French geologist and paleontologist Joachim Barrande who did scientific research at this locale. His twenty two volume geological work titled *"Systeme Silurien du Centre de la Bohéme"*, and his collections and library were donated to the National Museum.

Since 1927 the rocky heights, south of the city overlooking the Vltava River, have been synonymous with Czech film, since the first film studios were constructed there

(1931–4). It soon became an exclusive art and film colony. The restaurant Terasa was built by producer Max Urban in 1929, and a swimming pool on the rocks nearby in 1930. Barrandov Film Studios officially began operation on February 20, 1933, founded by Urban and Miloš Havel, uncle of President **Václav Havel**. Czech film luminaries **Miloš Forman** and Jiří Menzel began their careers at Barrandov. Most Czech films were made here as well as numerous international co–productions. Traditionally, many prominent movie executives, directors, actors, writers and even diplomats have lived in Barrandov villas.

## ■ BEER AND BREWERIES ■

Prague is not only a town of important historical and cultural monuments but is also a town world famous for its beer and breweries. The first documentation of Prague's breweries comes from the end of the 11th century. Three centuries later, Czech beer was known as the best in Europe. To maintain its superior reputation,  King **Charles IV** forbade the export of Czech hops. During his reign there were 36 breweries in Prague. Beer–making was an important town privilege and economic element.

In the middle of the 19th century there were about 60 large and small breweries in and around Prague. Some streets are traditionally known for their excellent beer: Dlouhá Street contained the U Klouzorů, U Celestýnů, U Zlaté štiky, U Zeleného stromu, U Myslíků, U Fáfů, U Bonů breweries. On Na Poříčí Street people visited U Bucků, U Rozvařilů, and U Labutí breweries. On **Wenceslas Square** there were the breweries U Březinů, U Šenfloků, U Primasů, and U Turků. On Charles Square there was the Černý Brewery, which now exists as a restaurant called Černý Pivovar, and the U Seidlerů, U Šálků, U Palmů, U Virlů, and na Slovanech breweries.

At the end of the 19th century the council of Prague's Burgesses decided to build a main town brewery on the bank of the Vltava near Holešovice. The foundation stone

*Pub U Zlatého Tygra on January 11, 1994: B. Hrabal, presidents V. Havel and B. Clinton / Photo by Jiří Jírů*

was laid on April 9, 1895, by Prague's notables. The projected volume was to be 100,000 hecto–litres per year with a capacity of three times that volume. Permission was granted by Prague's municipal authority on July 30, 1895, that the symbol of Prague could be used for the beer's emblem.

Other famous present–day breweries include the Staropramen Brewery in Smíchov, and the Braník Brewery in Prague 4.

The most attractive brewery for tourists is the famous U Fleků, on Křemencova Street, established in 1499. After the Battle of White Mountain (1621) the pub was seized and closed. In 1762 it was reopened as a pub by Jakub and Dorothy Flekovi, and renamed after them. They began making their renowned dark beer again in 1834, which is still served, called bavarian, and is a rare leaven 13 degree beer. Its taste is influenced by four types of malt: Pilsen, Bavarian, Caramel, and Roasted Malt. The beer is not sold for use outside the pub.

The pub's patron's include not only working classes but also artists, writers, and actors. Famous actors such as Mošna, Vojan, writers such as **Neruda**, Tyl, Vrchlický and **Hašek** often drank at U Fleků. The pub is large , and contains rooms called "In the Suitcase", "Emauzy", "The Academy", "The Sausage", and "The Hop–Gardens".

Besides the U Fleků, other famous beer halls include the U Kalicha, near I.P. Pavlova, and also associated with Hašek's Schweik, the U Medvídků on Perštýn, the U Pinkasů on Jungmann Square, the U Schnellů in Malá Strana on Tomášská Street, the U Supa on Celetná Street, U Sv. Tomáše on Letenská Street in Malá Strana, U Zlatého Tygra on Husova, visited by **Bohumil Hrabal** and **Havel** (and U.S. President Bill Clinton), and also the U Labutí in Krč, near Thomayer Hospital, preferred by many beer afficionados.

# ■ LUDWIG VAN BEETHOVEN ■

"Remember this fellow!" exclaimed **Mozart**, the first time he heard the scowling, homely young pianist von Beethoven play, "They'll be talking about him someday!" Mozart was definitely right, van Beethoven's piano opened a new epoch in music history. Questions, rumours and half–truths are still abound from their meeting. Did the young Beethoven want only to show Mozart his compositions or did he seek him as teacher? It is no secret however that they were both Prague favorites.

In Little Quarter beneath **Prague Castle** at the corner of Lázeňská Street at Malostranské náměstí, the City of Prague has erected a plaque commemorating Beethoven's stay. The building formerly housed a famous hotel called U Zlatého Jednorožce (At the Golden Unicorn). Both Mozart, invited by Count Lichnowski, and Beethoven stayed in this hotel during separate visits. Beethoven played there, and, when he was 26 years old, probably composed *"Ah, Perfido, Spergiuro,"* a concert tune for Josefina Claryova, a beautiful aristocrat. Beethoven, who also visited the baths in the towns of Teplice in northern Bohemia, and Hrádek near Opava won the hearts of Praguers by playing in the Konvict concert hall. The Count Clam–Gallas showed Beethoven the same hospitality the Dušek couple had shown Mozart, by providing him a haven in which to work, a classic **Baroque** palace located at No. 20 Husova Street in Old Town.

## ■ BERTRAMKA ■

Bertramka is a lovely villa in the hills of Smíchov once owned by František Xavier Dušek (a composer, virtuouso, and teacher) and his wife Josefína (a singer), famous because **Mozart** stayed there as the couple's guest during his visits to Prague. It's cozy interiors and peaceful chestnut orchard provided Mozart a working haven where he finished the prelude to "**Don Giovanni**", and where he wrote *"Bella mia fiamma, addio"* (or Farewell My Beautiful Flame), in appreciation of his hostess Josefína. The

*Bertramka
– the W. A. Mozart
Museum*

villa is converted to a Mozart Museum (located at No. 169
Mozartova Street, Prague 5– Smíchov) and outside, in his
favorite orchard, a bust of Mozart was erected commemorating his stay at Bertramka.

Mozart's stays in Prague were pleasing and he often
said: "These dear Praguers understand me...", and though
he spent a relatively short period of his short life in Prague,
the Praguers and Mozart seemed to connect well, and the
Praguers particularly understood and appreciated his art.

Another memorable locale Mozart frequented over two
hundred years ago in Prague is the **Stavovské–Estates
Theatre**, a classicism building in the old town, adjacent
to the **Carolinum**. The theatre is famous as the site of the
world premiere of *"Don Giovanni"*, considered the opera
of operas, which was written with Prague in mind. Coming and going between the theatre and Bertramka for
rehearsals, walking at night through the center along
Fruitmarket, lent a certain romance to the summer he
spent in Prague creating *Don Giovanni.*

## ■ FRANTIŠEK BÍLEK AND SYMBOLISM ■

Symbolism is an artistic movement that uses symbols to
manifest the artists intangible world, his dreams, his vi-
sions, his truths, and in the Czech tradition sometimes
incorporates **Art Nouveau** styles as well. Symbolist art
caught on in Bohemia about ten years after the movement
was developed in France, in the late 1800's. Symbolism
influenced many leading literary and art figures including: the painter F. Kupka (who later became an adherent
of abstract art), painter J. Preisler, and graphic artist
V. Preissig. It was practiced until World War I.

The sculptor František Bílek (1872–1941) is considered
one of the most important Czech Symbolists. Bílek first
studied painting at the Prague Academy of Fine Arts and
then sculpture at the Collarosi Academy in Paris from
1891 to 1892.

Bílek's work was generally suppressed after his death

until the 1960's, when there was a re-evaluation of symbolist and Art Nouveau artists, and Bílek's powerful ability
to express the spiritual and religious aspects of man, his
intuition and ecstacies, was recognized. His work is now
found in front of the Old-new **synagogue** in the old town
(a sculpture from 1905 called *"Moses Thinking of Adam"*),
and is collected and exhibited at the Bílek Villa (on
Mickiewiczova Street), the artist's former residence and
studio located near the **Renaissance**-style Belvedere Chateau and **Prague Castle**. The villa, completed in 1911, was
designed by Bílek to express his innermost aspirations as
a symbolist and religious artist, and to serve as a living
space and studio as well as a gallery and temple of art.

## ■ TYCHO DE BRAHE ■

The famous Danish astronomer Tycho de Brahe (1546–1601) came to
Prague after losing the sponsorship
of King Frederick II's court. He was
invited by Emperor **Rudolph II**,
who established an observatory for
him near the **Prague Castle**. Rudolph also granted de Brahe permission to invite **Johannes Kepler**,
another famous astronomer, to work
with him there. Tycho de Brahe enjoyed great support
of the Emperor at the court.

   He died October 24, 1601 in Prague and was buried in
Týn Cathedral at Staroměstské náměstí (Old Town Square). The location of his actual final resting place became
questionable however after the Battle of White Mountain
in 1620; the battle resulted in mass re-Catholization
throughout the Czech lands, and some believed his body
had been removed from the church around this time. This
question loomed larger as time went on until finally, three
centuries later, it prompted a detailed investigation of his
remnants. They were exhumed and de Brahe was identi-

fied by his telltale gold and silver nose cone. The nose piece was acquired as a result of a duel he had participated in, in Rostock in 1566, with a Danish noble who grazed away the tip of Brahe's nose with his weapon. Thus the enigma of his resting place was resolved, reaffirming his position at the Týn Cathedral.

When he worked in Prague (1599–1601) he lived in a **Renaissance** house at the Prague Castle at Pohořelec (on Parléřova Street) with Kepler. Presently this house is a school, commemorated with a monument to both astronomers.

## ■ MAX BROD ■

Max Brod (1884–1968) was probably one of the greatest publicists of modern Czech and Prague culture. A versatile personality, he wore the hat of writer, philosopher, playwright, theatre and music critic, translator, musician, editor, and active cultural organizer.

He was born in Prague at No. 1031 Haštalská Street, attending Piarist school at No. 1 Panská Street, accompanied by his friends **E.E. Kisch** and **Franz Werfel**. He later attended the German gymnasium on Štěpánská Street and studied law at Prague University, where he became friends with **Franz Kafka**. One of the first to recognize Kafka's talent, he became Kafka's confidante, publisher and enthusiastic critic. He discovered Leoš Janáček and stimulated the reputation of **Jaroslav Hašek**. He dramatized Hašek's Schweik for the Berlin stage in 1928, which was directed by Erwin Piscator and starred the famous actor Max Pallenberg.

Max Brod became a legend for not carrying out the wishes of his best friend Kafka, who directed him on his deathbed to burn all his writings; instead, by preserving them, Brod contributed to man's literary treasures. Brod

was a leading personality of a new artistic generation before the First World War and remained significant in Prague until forced to escape from the <u>Nazis</u> in 1939. He settled in Tel Aviv, Palestine, where he worked as a dramaturge in the Habimah Theatre. He was last in Prague in
1964 to give a lecture in Czech about Kafka.

Brod's notable literary work includes the trilogy *"Ein
Kampf und die Wahrheit"* – the novels *"Tycho Brahes Weg
zum Gott"* (1915), *"Reubeni, Fürst der Juden"* (1925), and
*"Galilei in Gefangenschaft"* (1948). Interesting reading
about cultural happenings and the eclectic atmosphere
of prewar Prague are related in Brod's essays *"Prager
Sternenhimmel"* (1913), *"Streitbares Leben"* (1960), and
*"Der Prager Kreis"* (1966). The latter memoir describes
the Prague–German literary circle in the early 1900's,
gathered about Kafka, Brod, Oscar Baum, and Felix
Weltsch. As Brod admits "We could consider Prague itself
as our teacher and program: its streets, inhabitants, history, the urban and nearby rural surroundings, the forests
and villages we zealously traversed, the city and its strug-
gles, its three nationalities, and its messianic hope in many hearts."

## ■ E.F. BURIAN, THEATRE D 34
## AND CZECH AVANT–GARDE THEATRE ■

As Berlin's avant–garde theatre is linked with Brecht and
Piscator, Prague's avant–garde theatre is intimately linked
with director E.F. Burian (1904–59) and his theatre "D 34".

The Czech avantgarde theatre between the Great Wars
featured three significant personalities: directors Jindřich
Honzl and Jiří Frejka who in 1925–6 founded the legendary "Osvobozené Divadlo" (Liberated Theatre, later linked
with author/actors Jiří Voskovec and Jan Werich), and
E.F. Burian, who achieved considerable international recognition. The young musician and dadaist eccentric began his career beside Frejka at the Theatre <u>Dada</u> in
1927–8. He also founded and led his own recitational

group VoiceBand in 1927, and, later, his own theatre (D 34), which became well known not only in Czech circles but also in the annals of modern European theatre.

By 1941, when the D 34 ensemble was disbanded by the **Nazis**, Burian had presented a revolutionary repertoire staged in a unique synthetic style that included: Brecht's *Beggar's Opera*, *Vojna (War)* – a ballet and voice band collage based upon folk poetry, a dramatized version of **Hašek**'s *"Good Soldier Schweik"*, Pushkin's *"Eugene Onegin"*, a **surrealistic** *Hamlet the Third*, works of Czech avant-garde authors V. Nezval and A. Hoffmeister, and so on.

*E. F. Burian*
*(1904–59)*

*Drawing by*
*Adolf Hoffmeister*

*Jiří Frejka, E.F. Burian and actresses of the Theatre DADA (1927)*

After returning from Nazi concentration camps, Burian succumbed to Stalinist terror and became sympathetic to the socialist theatre. After he died in 1959, the D 34 Theatre renamed itself the E.F. Burian Theatre. After the recent reconstruction of the theatre, a functionalist architectural gem, it has been renamed Archa (Ark), and now hosts various artistic groups. It's address is No. 26 Na Poříčí, Praha 1.

E.F. Burian was also an agile author and theoretician, whose works from the 1920's and 30's, such as *"On Modern Russian Music"*, *"Polydynamics"*, *"Jazz"*, *"Negro Dance"*, *"Sweep the Stage"*, *"Theatre of Labor"* are greatly admired today.

## ■ CAFES ■

The pastime of enjoying coffee at small restaurants became popular in the 18th century in France, Italy and Austria, and it is generally believed that the first cafe established in Prague is At the Golden Snake on Karlova Street, ca. 1714, built by Georgius Damascenus. Others contend that At the Three Ostriches near the Charles Bridge in Malá Strana (now a hotel) was the first cafe.

In 1777, the cafe At the Red Eagle was established at No. 20 Celetná, which was frequented by numerous writers and actors, such as J.K. Tyl, **F. Palacký**, K.J. Erben, and K.H. Mácha, in the first half of the 19th century. In his book Praga Magica, **Angelo Maria Ripellino**, reflects on the importance of cafes in the intellectual societies of Prague. One of the most famous and popular was the Cafe Union on Národní Street which many intellectuals enjoyed, but it was closed by the Gestapo in 1941 and later demolished in 1949. The Albatros children's book publishing house now occupies the former site of the cafe.

**Rilke** wrote of the National Cafe on Národní třída, and **Kafka** and **Brod** enjoyed Louvre on Národní třída and Cafe Arco at No. 16 Hybernská (where Karl Kraus called the customers Arconauts and the mix of Czechs, Germans and Jews "Es werfelt, und brodet, und kafkat, und kischt."
At Cafe Arco customers included the artists Willy Nowak, Bedřich Feigl, Georg Kars, and Alfred Justitz. German artists frequented the Continental too, where a seat was reserved daily for Gustav Meyrink and his associates.

Prague is rich with **Secese** (**Art Nouveau**) cafes.
The best include Hotel Europa on **Wenceslas Square**, Cafe

Nouveau in **Obecní Dům** on Náměstí Republiky, Hanavský Pavilion in Letenské Orchards, and the cafe of Hotel Paříž, the setting for **Bohumil Hrabal**'s book "I served the King of England".

Over one hundred cafes closed during the time of **Communism**, most have not reopened. Famous cafes such as Cafe Slavia, built in 1863 across from the **National Theatre**, and Malostranské Cafe on Malostranské náměstí are still being remodelled. **Jaroslav Seifert** wrote a famous poem called "Cafe Slavia" which describes the entrance of **Apollinaire** into the circle of Czech avant– garde. The Cafe Slavia is where the National Theatre actors gathered, particularly in the 1960's, especially famous was the table of **Jiří Kolář** whose admirers included **Václav Havel**.

---

■ **CAROLINUM** ■

If one goes from the Old Town Square via Železná Street one will see on ones left, at No. 16 Ovocný Trh (Fruit Market), one of Prague's most interesting Middle Age monuments, the Carolinum.

The building, originally occupied by master minter Johlin Rothlev of Kutná Hora, became one of the oldest university buildings in Europe when it was affiliated with the Charles University, established in 1348. The renowned scholars of this period, who formerly had presented their lectures in churches, monasteries and private houses, were able to teach at the Carolinum. Early on, the Czechs and German portions of the population vied for control of the school, but after 1638 it was controlled by **the Jesuits** (formerly more active at the nearby **Clementinum**). In 1784, schooling at the Carolinum changed over from Latin to the German language, and, in 1881, the university was subdivided into German and Czech departments. It was closed during World War II by the **Nazis**, and afterwards it was utilized only by Czechs.

The Carolinum's **Baroque** facade is the result of remodelling in 1718 by the Prague architect František Kaňka, who also created the beautiful portal at the front entrance facing Železná Street. The **Gothic** oriel window at the corner of Ovocný Trh and Železná, containing the coats of arms of Rothlev, of the Archbishop Jan of Jenštejn, and of Bohemia and Moravia, is actually from the original structure. Although the ground floor is nearly original too, the first floor underwent a major reconstruction in 1946–50, to accomodate modern schooling needs (i.e., the Great Hall), under the supervision of architect Jaroslav Fragner. He also worked on the portion of the Carolinum facing Ovocný Trh, where a new entrance and office buildings were constructed in 1969. In 1975, a fountain with lions designed by V. Makovský and cut from stone by Stanislav Hanzík was placed at the front of the building in accordance with a plan by J. Fragner.

## ■ CASANOVA ■

Giovanni Giacomo de Seingalt (1725–98), commonly known as Casanova, was an Italian writer and adventurer infamous for his scandalous affairs and wanderlust. For a time he lived in northern Bohemia in the Duchcov Castle, and he visited Prague a number of times. According to the book *"Amadeus and Casanova"* by Louis Fürnberg, it is believed that Casanova attended a ball with **Mozart** in January, 1787, at the Brettfeld Palace at No. 240/33 Nerudova Street, and that he also attended the opening of Mozart's opera of operas *"Don Giovanni."* Alfred Meissner further relates (in his book *"Roccocobilder"*) a prank played on Mozart at the time he was finishing the opera's overture: his friends led him to a pavilion, gave him inspiration "with sticks" and locked him there. Casanova was able to obtain the keys and free Mozart from his pavilion prison. If Casanova had any other piquant profligations in Prague, they have gone to the grave with the participants.

# ■ CHARLES IV – CAROLUS ■

The Czech, Roman king and emperor, son of John of Luxembourg and Elizabeth of Přemysl, Charles IV was born
on May 14, 1316, and died on November 29, 1378.

Charles IV was educated in France, in 1334 became
margrave of Moravia and in 1341 was the co-governor
of Bohemia. In 1346, he was elected Roman–German king
and, in the same year, after his father's death, was elected
Czech king. In 1355, he was coronated as an emperor in
Rome.

Charles IV greatly improved the quality of the Czech
state by initiating large construction projects and
strengthening the position of the church. Due to his
incentive, the Archbishop's post was established by
the Pope in Prague in 1344.

Under Charles' rule, Prague became the residential
town of the Empire. Brandenburg and numerous other foreign territories were annexed by Charles. The quality
of political life was enhanced by a Golden Bull attained by
Charles IV for the Czech lands.

Charles IV was one of the most highly educated men in
Europe at that time. He knew five languages and was very
knowledgable in the arts and sciences, he had literary
gifts (he wrote his biography– *"Vita Caroli"*), he was an
outstanding soldier and statesman, a truly multifaceted talent.

His rule was extremely important from a political,
cultural, and economic viewpoint for the Czech nation.
Prague was to have become the heart and treasury of
Europe, a jewel of natural beauty interwoven with
masterpieces of construction under Charles. He was a collector, sponsor, and lover of art. Prague, in Charles time,
was the place where great artists such as Francesco
Petrarca, his friend and poet, and another Italian,
adventurer Cola di Rienzi, lived.

When Charles was seventeen he arrived in Prague and
began remodelling **Prague Castle**, which had burned in

*Charles Bridge*

1304. In 1344, in connection with establishing the post of Prague's Archbishop (Arnošt of Pardubice), the foundation stone for the Cathedral of St. Vitus was laid. In 1347, the monastery, Na Slovanech (Emauzy) was begun and, in 1348, he founded the New Town of Prague, his most substantial project. At the same time, Prague's university, the **Carolinum** was established, the first of its kind in central

Europe. Two months later Matthew of Arras was commissioned to build Karlstein Castle. Also in 1347, the Cathedral of the Virgin Mary of Snows, the Church of Assumption of the Virgin Mary, and of Charles the Great, in Karlov, the monastery of St. Ambrose (1355), today the House of Hybern (U Hybernů). He also established the Charles Bridge in 1357 and many other construction projects. He provided urban planning for Prague, for example the radial avenues extending from the former gates, and his plan still influences the transportation network in the centre.

In the current districts of Vinohrady, Smíchov, Košíře, Dejvice, and on the slopes of the Vltava, he established vineyards. He also founded a menagerie with lions and tigers, known today as the Lion Yard, in the Stag Moat (Jelení příkop) he kept other exotic animals, he founded gardens, parks and ponds. He developped the Vltava for navigation.

For his achievements in the Czech lands he is generally known as "the father of the country".

## ■ CHURCHES ■

The most important and numerous Church in Prague is the Catholic Church, whose Primate resides at Hradčanské náměstí at the Archbishop's Palace. The Ecumenical Council of Churches is another important Church institution in Prague (at No. 13 Vítkova, Prague 8–Karlín). Other organizations acting in Prague include Unity of Baptist Brethren (No. 10 Na Topolce, Prague 4–Nusle), Adventist Church (No. 50 Zálesí, Prague 4–Lhotka), Church of Brethren (No. 15, Soukenická, Prague 1–Nové Město), Church of Czech Evangelic Brethren (No 9 Jungmannova, Praha 1–Nové Město), Czechoslovak Hussites Church (No. 5 V.V. Kujbyševa, Prague 6–Dejvice), Methodist Evangelic Church (No. 19 Ječná, Prague 2–Nové Město), Orthodox Church (No. 6 V jámě, Prague 1, Nové Město), Uniate Church (No 1 Karlova, Prague 1–Staré Město),

*Monastery of the Knights of the Cross*

Slovak Evangelic Church (No 8 Čajkovského, Prague 3–Žižkov), Old Catholic Church (No. 4 Blodkova, Prague 3–Žižkov), Unity of Brethren (No 5 Hálkova, Prague 2–Nové Město) and the Religious Society of Czechoslovak Unitarians (No 8 Karlova, Prague 1–Staré Město).

In Prague there are a total of 220 liturgical buildings, including 97 churches, 15 chapels, and some rectory and tabernacle buildings. The oldest and most precious church monuments are rotundas (circular **Romanesque** sacral buildings).

Historial circumstances have dictated a preponderance of Catholic churches in Prague, and services are regularly performed in most of them.

## ■ CIMRMAN ■

This chapter should rightly be titled "Jára da Cimrman or Towards Prague's History of Mystification," because it describes a magical phenomenon deeply embedded in Czech literature and culture. This genial character of the Czech imagination, who like Leonardo da Vinci, has allegedly affected numerous scientific and artistic events in Czech history. The mystic emerged at the second half

*Authors and actors of Jára Cimrman's Theatre:*
*Z. Svěrák and L. Smoljak*

of the 1960's at the time of political détente which resulted in the "**Prague Spring**" of 1968. In a radio program called Winery at the Spider several editors such as Zdeněk Svěrák and Jiří Šebánek, writers, including Josef Škvorecký, and **jazz** musicians met to create the fictitious world of Cimrman, a genial jack–of–all–trades. Within a backdrop of secessionist and idyllic provincial Bohemia of the Austrian–Hungarian Empire, Cimrman longed to show the Kaisers of Vienna and the whole world what could be accomplished by a clever Czech fellow.

The pilot project was transferred from radio to a theatre ensemble called Divadlo Járy Cimrmana, led by author/actors Zdeněk Svěrák and Ladislav Smoljak, and staged continuously, incredibly, since 1967. The ensemble was first hosted at the Malostranská Beseda at the Malostranské náměstí, then the Reduta **Jazz** Club, then at the **Divadlo Na Zábradlí** (**Theatre on the Balustrade**), and elsewhere, and now resides at the Žižkovské Theatre.

During the 1970's and 80's this literary and theatrical phenomenon became widely popularized, not just because the cycle of plays were successful on LP's and at the movies, but because this tight–lipped, grouchy, pig–headed and "genial" sour puss was viewed by the general public as an analogy of a cult of hated **communist** dictators like Lenin and Stalin, who had also originally been presented as Jack–of–all–Trades, talking serious–faced on any and all topics.

The literary nature of this phenomenon, immensely possessed of cultivation and an extraordinary sense of humour, understandable particularly in Central Europe, suggests that the work of Mr. Cimrman, more precisely Svěrák and Smoljak, will become appreciated abroad as is another classic mystic, **Hašek**'s soldier Schweik.

The Theatre of Jára Cimrman resides in Žižkovské Theatre, No. 5 Štítného Street, Prague 3.

# ■ CLASSICISM AND EMPIRE ■

Classicism and Empire dates back to the second half of the eighteenth century up to the 1830's. Classicism covers the entire period while Empire relates only to a part, the so–called First Empire of France.

Classicism represents a style which results from studies of the antique and theoretical interpretations of J.J. Winkelmann, replacing the **Baroque**, and thus the calm facades of certain Classicist houses containing Baroque elements such as pilasters and cornices. In general, however, the architecture was increasingly based upon the harmonic use of constructive elements. Examples include the Teresian wing of the **Prague Castle** which surround three yards of the western part. Classicist painters and sculptors fully utilized antique motifs as seen in the paintings and drawings of the first director of the Prague Academy of Creative Art, Josef Bergler (1753–1829).

Unique "galleries" of Classicist sculptoral art may be found at two Prague cemeteries, Olšanské Cemetery over Vinohrady and Malostranský Cemetery in Košíře. From Olšanské Square one may enter into to the circular Church of St. Roch which neighbours the Lapidarium which, in turn, houses many classicist sculptures of Prague. At Plzeňská Street one finds the old Malostranský Cemetery which might be considered a museum of buried Classicist Funereal sculpture as well. Dominant is a monument with a kneeling figure of Passau Bishop, Leopold Thun–Hohenstein, made from cast iron in 1830–31 from a model by Prague sculptor Václav Prachner. Another interesting thing about this cemetery is that **Mozart**'s friends, the singer Josephina Duškova and her husband composer F.X. Dušek, are also buried here.

Indeed, Mozart's activities are closely linked to the Stavovské Theatre (**Estates Theatre**), an exemplary Classicist building (1781–1783) of Antonin Haffenecker. This architect secured his place in the history of Prague's architecture by also designing Swerts–Sporck Palace

at No. 1036 Hybernská Street. The Palace was begun
in 1783 simultaneously with the Classicist remodelling
of a large portion of the buildings lining this street. Today
the Palace houses the American Cultural Centre.

Other Classicist structures include: the swimming facility near the Svatopluk Čech bridge in front of the Hotel
Intercontinental; Slovanský House on Na Příkopě; a large
part of the Karlín district, including the large Invalidovna
complex; the unique Masaryk Railway Station, representative of an industrial application; and houses along the
Smetana embankment between **National Theatre** and the
Charles Bridge. All these reflect a compositional ideal,
beauty of harmony, and classical patterns.

Examples of Empire architecture include the former
Customs office building, currently occupied by the exhibi-
tion hall "U Hybernů" at the Powder Tower, the Church of
The Holy Cross on Na Příkopě, and the Kinsky Pavilion on
**Petřín Hill**. They represent the last easily distinguishable
style characteristic of Europe in the nineteenth century.

## ■ CLEMENTINUM ■

The Clementinum was begun between 1638–40. Its construction required thirty houses to be demolished. It was
built as a **Jesuit** college. Carlo Lurago was its first architect, and he designed the Church of San Salvatore and the
portion of the school on Křížovnická Street (1653–60)
which made it the second largest building complex in Prague next to the **Prague castle**. Many architects followed,
as construction continued through the ages, such as František Kaňka who built the observatory tower (1721–3) and
the buildings on Mariánské Square.

In the 17th and 18th century the Clementinum represented one of the most important learning centres of
Europe, boasting many foreign academics and a famous
theatre. The prosperous Clementinum contained five
courtyards and four churches, utilized today by the State
Library. The original library of **Charles IV**, which the Je-

suits maintained and added to, was further increased after 1773, the year the Jesuits were restricted in the Czech lands, when the libraries of other Jesuit facilities were consolidated at the Clementinum. It now contains an enviable book collection that includes over five thousand handmade medieval books. During 1928–30, a large study hall was added to the **Baroque** building in the second courtyard, which modernized the learning centre.

The Clementinum administers Saint Kliment Church, Vlašská Chapel, and San Salvatore Church. The Clementinum may also be accessed near Charles Bridge. The study hall, the hall of mirrors where concerts are held, and certain other interiors are open to the public.

*Clementinum*

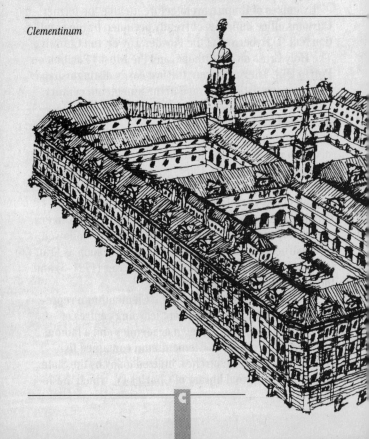

# ■ COMENIUS – JAN ÁMOS KOMENSKÝ ■

Jan Ámos Komenský (or Comenius, 1592–1670), an outstanding theoretician and practical pedagogue, was a very important figure in Czech culture. His work in educational programs provided the first foundations for schooling around the world. He was also a prestigious philosopher, social and religious thinker, and promoter of the Czech language. After graduating from evangelic schools at Herborn and Heidelberg, he taught at the School of Czech Brethren at Přerov. He was ordained and as a representative of the Brethren Unity, he was forced to leave the Czech realm in 1628 during the counter–reformation. He first ventured to Lešno, Poland, then to England and Swe-

den, and then took up residence in Amsterdam until his death. He is buried in Naarden, Netherlands.

Komenský's most famous works include allegories *"Labyrint of the World and Paradise of the Heart"*, *"Via Lucis"*, *"Opera didactica omnia"*, *"Janua linguarum reserata"*, *"Orbis pictus"*, *"Didactica magna"*, *"Lux in tenebris"*, etc.

*Comenius*

He is commemorated with statues by **František Bílek**, located in front of Bílek's villa (at Mickiewiczova Street). The Pedagoguist Museum of Jan Ámos Komenský is housed at **Wallenstein Palace** – No 4 Valdštejnské náměstí, Prague 1–Malá Strana, which displays the programs and methods initiated and developed by the great teacher.

## ■ COMMUNISM AND PRAGUE ■

For forty two years, between 1948 and the Velvet Revolution of 1989, Prague was imprinted with the names, statues, buildings, schools, etc., as well as the ideas, habits and methods of Communism.

One of the largest physical monuments of Communism was the Central Committee of the Communistic Party of Czechoslovakia, situated on the Ludvíka Svobody waterfront, a huge building originally designed for the Ministry of Transport (and now again occupied the Ministry). The nearby 330 metre Těšnov Tunnel was built in 1977–80 to divert traffic and quieten the streets adjacent to the Communist Committee building, so their meetings were not disturbed by the traffic.

The sanctuary of Communism was the Mausoleum on Vítkov Hill, designed after the Tomb of Lenin, for preservation of the first Communist President's body Klement Gottwald who was one of the primary leaders of the 1948 putsch and who was responsible for the death of many people during the purges in the 1950's.

With respect to law enforcement there are two main buildings of interest: the Communist Ministry of the Interior, designed and built in a modern architectural style in the 1930's, which contained official's offices and served as a large detention centre and interrogation centre; and the main police station on Bartolomějská Street in the Old Town. Some of the elder liberal thinking Praguers still become nervous when they are near these buildings.

Former Communist museums included the V.I. Lenin Museum on Hybernská Street established to commemorate the visit of Lenin in 1912, and now rented by the Socialist Democratic Party to the American Embassy (American Cultural Centre), and the Klement Gottwald Museum at No. 29 Rytířská under **Wenceslas Square**, converted back to bank (Česká spořitelna ). Although "the father of Communism" Karl Marx visited in 1874 and 1875, no museum was built in his honour.

The prominent Communist leaders occupied villas in Prague 6 and certain hotels such as Hotel Praha, in Prague 6, and Grand Hotel Bohemia at the present time, in the Old Town. They also had their own hospitals and their own stores forbidden to the average Party member and man on the street. For the average citizen they constructed massive prefabricated concrete panel housing complexes called "paneláks" that made up entire suburbs. The Communists also had two large prisons (Pankrác and Ruzyně) in Prague.

Perhaps the most absurd monument of Communism was the **Stalin Memorial**, unfortunately destroyed after the Twentieth Meeting of the Soviet Communist Party. The most glaring architectural mistake of Communist times is the Hotel International in Prague 6, built between 1956–7, luckily situated in a valley, however, so as not to interfere with the local panorama. The Hotel Jalta was also built at this time in the same style on **Wenceslas Square**. Large student dormitories in Podolí– Prague 4

and in Jarov– Prague 3, and the School of Politics in Vokovice– Prague 6 (called by Praguers "the Sorbonne of Vokovice") were also built by the Communists. Luckily many
of the gigantic projects on the Communist drawing boards
were not realized due to lack of funding.

After the Brussels Expo of '58, the Czechoslovakian pavilion was erected at the Výstaviště **exhibition grounds**
and the Expo restaurant was placed on Letná Hill which
influenced the architects to diminish the scale of their
work, closing the chapter on Historicism and Monumenta-
lism.

# ■ CONTEMPORARY ARCHITECTURE ■

After 1948 when the **Communist** government came to power in Czechoslovakia, the Prague architects found unfa-
vorable conditions to pursue their work in comparision
to the pre–World War II period of a democratic republic.
Under the Communists contact with Western architects
was considered ideologically disruptive. At the same time,
architects were hindered by a construction slowdown,
especially in the last twenty years (during which time only
ugly panel–type apartments were built). All architecturally
significant buildings created during this period represent
an immense endeavor in the face of resistance seldom
confronted by Western architects.

Some Western visitors are attracted to architecture
of the hard–line Stalinist era (1950–56) such as Hotel International at Podbaba in Prague 6, or the more cultivated
Hotel Jalta at **Wenceslas Square**, by architect Antonín
Tenzer.

Since the 1960's, Prague architects have attempted to
incorporate the Internationalistic style which influences
the design of a large portion of new construction even today. Architecturally significant works incorporating these
ideas include the Macromolecular Institute at Heyrovské-
ho náměstí, by Karel Prager (1959–64), New Airport at Ruzyně by Karel Filsak's team (1964–66), Kotva department

store at náměstí Republiky by the Machonin couple'
(1966–74), the interiors of the Prague metro (under construction since 1969), and administrative buildings of State Foreign Trade Enterprises such as Motokov at Pankrác
(1973–76), Koospol at Vokovice (1974–77), and Kovo at Holešovice (1974–77).

Beside this more or less official Prague architecture,
other architectural designs emerged whose designers were not afraid to use topical incentives from the West or
contemplate them in their work. The new lobby at the
main rail station (Wilson Station) was built in this vein,
designed by architects Bočan, Danda, Šrámková and Šrámek (1972–77). The lobby has a smartly shaped interior
in high–tech style, the front of it imitating the late stages
of Mies van der Rohe in a post–modernist spirit. This
post–modernist thinking was also displayed in another
work by Šrámková and Šrámek in the design of the administrative building of ČKD (a large engineering company)
at Wenceslas Square (1976–85). Another historical building is the Máj department store now owned by K–Mart at
Národní třída, by architects Eisler, Masák, and Rajniš
(1972–74), designed with high–tech tendencies, hinting
at Neo–functionalism.

The young generation of architects are characterized
by an effort to utilize the rough and cumbersome panel
technology in a positive architectural theme. Architects
thus oriented began as Neo–functionalists in the 1970's,
however, step–by–step matured toward more romantic
forms. This is true of Jan Línek and Vlado Milunič, who
designed the pensioner's home at the streets Rektorská,
Čimická and Donovalská, and the team, Brix–Králíček
–Kotík, who are designing public facilities complementing
the housing complexes at Lužiny and Stodůlky.

■ **CUBISM** ■

Cubism is an artistic style developed by such artists as
Pablo Picasso and Braque between 1907 and 1914. Picasso

was influenced by African statues and by Cezanne's analytical constructions of shape and space, courageously liberating form from its exterior reality.

Picasso's Avignon's Misses, from 1907, opened the French Cubist epoch of painting, also called the Negro Era. In 1910 the movement progressed to analytical Cubism, evolving in 1912 to synthetic Cubism which continued into the 1920's. The poet **Apollinaire** helped the Cubist movement involve an entire generation.

Dr. Vincenc Kramář in 1910, was the among the first to promote the theories of Cubism outside of France, and, along with American writer Gertrude Stein, German art historian Wilhelm Uhde, and the Russian art dealer Ščukin, became one of the first collectors of Cubist art. Between the years 1910 and 1913, the Czech doctor collected twenty Picasso paintings, numerous graphics, sketches and statues, and also important examples of Braque and Derain. In 1911 he exhibited the paintings in Prague for the benefit of Czech painters such as Emil Filla, Bohumil Kubišta, Antonín Procházka, Vincenc Beneš, Josef Čapek, and others from The Group of Artists (1911–14), and also for architects and sculptors, such as **Otto Gutfreund**. Many of these artists exhibited Cubist

*Famous Cubist architecture:*
*apartment building below Vyšehrad*

–influenced works in Berlin at Sturm Gallery in 1913.

The acceptance of the Cubist movement in the Czech lands is revealed by the numerous Cubist–style constructions built between 1911 and 1914. Prague was probably one of the greatest admirers of Cubist art and architecture.

The most important and famous Cubist architecture in Prague includes: The House At the Black Godmother, No. 567 Celetná Street, and a duplex at No. 4–6 Tychonova Street at the **Prague Castle**, both designed by Josef Gočár and built in 1911–2; The Diamant House, No. 4 Spálená, built in 1912 by Josef Chochol who also designed a group of apartment buildings below Vyšehrad (including a triplex at No.6–10 Rašínovo nábřeží, a residence at No. 30 Neklanová Street and at No. 3 Libušina Street); the Ďáblice cemetery with its interesting Cubist entrance was built by Vlastislav Hofman in 1912–3; several houses on E.Krásnohorské Street near Pařížská Street were designed by Otakar Novotný, who also designed the **Mánes** building on the river front and a Cubist lamp–post in front of No. 14 Jungmannovo náměstí behind the Baťa shoe–store. Czech artists also designed Cubists lamps, furniture, mirrors, clocks, and vases and Cubism influenced graphics and stage design. Publications and international exhibitions often recognize the importance of the abundant and unique Cubist art in Prague.

# ■ CZECH PHILHARMONIC ■

Near the Charles Bridge, with its foundations submerged in the Vltava, there is an important building– it houses **Smetana**'s Museum. And just a few minutes away, just past the Mánes' statue and the Mánes Bridge, another great building– its wide stairs dangerously overcrowded with music patrons– the Rudolphinum (or House of Artists), the home of the Czech Philharmonic, where venues of **Mozart** and Smetana often resound. Its notable accoustics and recording qualities draw Prague's music fans to the large hall to hear symphonic concerts and chamber music recitals. The main attraction is the Czech Philharmonic, once conducted by the likes of Talich, Kubelík, Ančerl, Neumann, respected and admired worldwide, and its concerts are a pillar of Prague's rich music scene. Each May, the building bustles with activity when the international music **festival** "Prague Spring" is held there.

The Czech Philharmonic was founded in Prague in 1894. It comprises the Czech Philharmonic orchestra, the Prague Philharmonic ensemble, Kühn's children's ensemble, chamber music groups, and soloists. The Symphonic Orchestra was formed at the end of the century as well, by members of the National Theatre Orchestra in a group called for Promotion of Musicial Art in Prague.

The Czech Philharmonic began its artistic activity on January 4, 1896, with a concert conducted by **Antonín Dvořák**. Today's leading conductor is Gerd Albrecht, also head of the Hamburg Orchestra. Other guest conductors include: O. Klemperer, A. Pedrotti, W. Sawallisch, H. von Karajan, L. Matačič, K. Böhm, G. Rozhdestvenskiy, S.Baudo, L. Bernstein, R. Kubelík, and so on. The orchestra has played in more than 30 countries on four continents.

---

### ■ KAREL ČAPEK ■

Karel Čapek (1890–1938), whose life is closely associated with Prague, was a very important Czech humanist, writer, dramatist, essayist and journalist. He worked with his brother, Josef, who was an equally talented artist and writer, and both were early supporters of **Cubism**. They lived together, from 1907, first at No. 532/11 Říční Street in Malá Strana, then in a stylish duplex (villa) they constructed

*Karel Čapek and Josef Čapek*

at No. 1853/28 Úzká Street, Praha 2 – Vinohrady. Here, between the World Wars, they hosted some of the most influential Czech and foreign intellectuals of the day – called Fridayers, because these politicians, philosophers, writers and artists met each Friday (President **T.G. Masaryk** regularly attended). He was also an avid gardener and maintained a beautiful garden at the villa which he describes in *"The Gardener's Year."*

Karel Čapek was an editor of Lidové noviny from 1921 to 1923, he worked as dramaturge and director at the Vinohrady Theatre, and as his international reputation grew he became chairman of the Czech Pen Club from 1925 to 1933. He gained local and international recognition first with his metaphysical treatises and science–utopian novels such as *"The Factory of Absolute"* and *"Krakatit"*, then with plays like *"From an Insects Life"* and *"R.U.R."*, and finally with such antiwar pieces as *"White Disease"*, *"Mother"*, and *"War of the Salamanders"*, written on the eve of World War II. Nazi collaborators made Čapek's final years miserable. He died on December 25, 1938. His brother Josef was sent to Nazi concentration camps and never returned.

## ■ ČINOHERNÍ KLUB – DRAMA CLUB ■

Theatre–goers interested in famous Prague drama and the ensembles which led a dramatic surge of Czech theatre across the European scene in the 1960's recall **Divadlo Na Zábradlí** (Theatre on the Balustrade), **Divadlo Za Branou** (Theatre Behind the Gate), Národní Divadlo (**National Theatre**), and the Činoherní Klub (Drama Club).

The Činoherní Klub has resided at No. 26 Ve Smečkách

Street, in a small theatre a few steps from **Wenceslas Square**, since its inception in 1964. It was founded by theatre theoretist and director Jaroslav Vostrý, accompanied by director Jan Kačer, director and dramatist Ladislav Smoček, and directors Evald Schorm and Jiří Menzel.

From its beginning the theatre emphasized the development of the actors' art, colourful and rich interpretations of Russian classics (Gogol, Chekhov, etc.), works of authors associated with the theatre such as Alena Vostrá, and Ladislav Smoček, then Harold Pinter, and M. Frayn, and dramatizations of beloved bohemian **Bohumil Hrabal**'s prosaic works including *"I Served the King of England"* and *"Tender Barbarian"*.

It was no accident that this center of theatre and cultural life became the headquarters of the Civic Forum, the most significant civic group of artists, students, dissidents, etc., gathering there on November 19, 1989, at the beginning of the so–called **Velvet Revolution**.

The ensemble which in the 1960's helped to establish the proverb "The Theatre God Has Settled in Prague" is now one of the most attractive drama groups of the chamber genre, particularly for youths.

# ■ DADA ■

One of the first international movements of modern art, between 1915 and 1923, dada was developed at Zürich's Cabaret Voltaire and in Paris, New York, in areas of Germany – Berlin, Hannover, and Cologne, and from these centres was incorporated piecemeal by Prague artists until becoming an integral part of **surrealism** here in the late 1920's. It's reception was sporadic and lukewarm.

In the early part of 1920, it was highly touted in the Czech press and the campaign whipped up a lot of public enthusiasm for the first meeting with the dadaists Raoul Hausmann, Richard Huelsenbeck, and Johannes Baader. On March 1, 1920, Hausmann and Huelsenbeck had a great success in the Hall of Corn Exchange at Senovážné náměstí, before an audience of 2500 people (despite the fact that Baader disappeared an hour before the exhibition, due to a case of the jitters, carrying off the lecture texts and the treasury), as they did the following day too, at the Hall of the Mozarteum (No. 30 Jungmannova Street). Prague Germans were particularly impressed and as early as April, 1920, they held a dadaist and futurist masked ball at Concordia (nowadays known as Slovanský dům, Na Příkopě Street).

In the summer of 1920, an ephemeral dadaist cell of Czech enthusiasts was founded (at its core were Artuš Černík, Zdeněk Kalista, and Jaromír Berák who published a pioneering essay called *Groove of Dadaism* in the magazine Den).

In 1921 the German dadaists (Hausmann, with Kurt Schwitters and Hannah Höch) presented themselves

*Raoul Hausmann, Richard Huelsenbeck and Johannes Baader*

in Prague again, at the Hall Urania on September 6–7. The same year Paul Klee exhibited his work, as the guest of the group Tvrdošíjní (Stubborns). In 1923 an exhibition called Bazaar of Modern Art, which hosted Man Ray, echoed a previous "Dada Messe" exhibition in Berlin. Domestic supporters of dada published some principles (poet František Halas in revue Pásmo; B. Václavek published an article called *"Creative Dada"* in Host magazine in 1925; **Karel Teige**, published *"On Humor, Clowns, and Dadaists"* in Host, 1926, and later separately in two volumes; and poet Vítězslav Nezval published an essay called "Dada and Surrealism" in the almanac Fronta 1927).

By the next time Kurt Schwitters visited Prague in 1926 the avant–garde theatre called Osvobozené had been established. Between 1926–29 the theatre presented authors such as Ribémont–Dessaignes, **Apollinaire**, Marinetti, Goll, Breton, Soupault, Cocteau, Jarry, all of the dadaist/surrealistic tree, at Umělecká Beseda in Malá Strana (today the hall presents only chamber music recitals). On May 20–21, 1926, Schwitters personally took part in his *"Evenings of Grotesques"* and in the winter of 1926–7 he exhibited at the Rudolphinum.

If dada featured not only provocation and scandals, but also mystification, then **Jaroslav Hašek** may be included.

And if we follow Karel Teige's definition of Dada as the "character of modern humour" we might include Osvobozené Theatre, with author/clowns Jiří Voskovec and Jan Werich, who developed dada–inspired humour in their first *Vest Pocket Revue* and subsequent works, and also the young eccentric musician and actor **E.F. Burian**, author of a dadaist poetry collection called *"Idioteon"*. E.F. Burian and Jiří Frejka, founder of Osvobozené Theatre, started the Dada Theatre in the spring of 1927, playing a repertoire that included Cocteau, Reverdy, and Schwitters (*"Schattenspiel"*). They performed in Umělecká Beseda and Divadlo Na Slupi, later demolished.

## ■ EMA DESTINNOVÁ ■

Ema Destinnová was born at No. 1526 Kateřinská Street, Prague 2 in 1878. Facing St. Nicholas Church in Malá Strana, is the house (formerly Kaiserstein Palace and now known as "At Petzold's", No. 23 Malostranské náměstí) where Ema Destinnová lived between tours until her death in 1930. This historic house once hosted 120 musicians, led by soprano Josefína Dušková, who played Rosetti's Requiem for the darling of Prague, **W.A. Mozart**.

She first gained fame in Bayreuth performing Wagner's operas at the age of 23, and performed at the Metropolitan Opera in New York at 30. She worked with musicians such as Richard Strauss, Giacomo Puccini, Enrico Caruso and the conductor Arturo Toscanini, and was celebrated in Germany, France, England and the United States. She was a renowned figure in Mozart's operas, playing Pamina in *the Magic Flute*, Contessa in the *Marriage of Figaro*, and Donna Anna in *Don Giovanni*.

Destinnová was an emancipated, fin–de–siecle artist of distinguished intellect, and was active as a poet, writer and translator of song texts. She collected art objects and books, and owned "Napoleon's Collection." Her activity against Austria during World War I resulted in her later move from Prague to her castle at Stráž nad Nežárkou.

# ■ DISCO ■

Discotheques became popular in Prague in the late 1960's, thanks to a few disc jockeys who played this style of dance music. Although the venue's addresses often changed, this form of youthful entertainment was not stopped by the Communist regime, and remained popular throughout the 1970's and 80's. Disco is still played in Prague, under more favorable conditions, in certain dance clubs and <u>rock cafes</u>. (A detail listing of discos is provided in the appendix.)

# ■ DIVADLO NA ZÁBRADLÍ
# – THEATRE ON THE BALUSTRADE ■

Located in the old part of Prague from the Charles Bridge past the <u>National Theatre</u> tucked away from the waterfront in cute little Anenské Square at No.5 is Divadlo na Zábradlí, Theatre on the Balustrade, considered the most progressive theatre in the Czech culture.

The theatre was established in 1958 by young Czech artists that included: Vladimír Vodička (director), Ladislav Fialka (pantomime artistic director), and Jiří Suchý and Ivan Vyskočil (actor/authors). It focused on both classic theatre and pantomime. Jan Grossman developed Jarry's *"King Ubu"* (1964), <u>Václav Havel</u>'s *"The Memorandum"*, and <u>Franz Kafka</u>'s *"The Trial"*, and Otomar Krejča, who directed Havel's *"The Garden Party"*, managed to bring Havel onboard as a playwright and dramaturge at Divadlo na Zábradlí.

At this time during the 1960's, the theatre played numerous absurdist pieces by such authors as Jarry, Ionesco, Beckett, Kafka, Havel, and Arrabal, and its employees included Václav Hudeček, Jaroslav Gillar, Jiří Menzel, Jaroslav Chundela, Evald Schorm, and Ivan Rajmont. They tried to maintain these standards throughout the 1970's and 1980's playing works such as Hrabal's *"Bambini di Praga"* and *"Noisy Loneliness"*, and authors Bond, Mrozek, Dostoevsky, Confortes, Albee, Vitrac, Camus, and resident playwright Karel Steigerwald.

The pantomime group of L. Fialka developed the the-
atre into a centre for pantomime arts and twice hosted the
International Pantomime Festival (in 1969 presenting
Marceau, Dimitri, Lecoq, and Molcho, and in 1971 with
Lecoq, Dimitri, Tomaszewski, and Byland).

In 1989 this theatre was deeply involved in the **Velvet
Revolution**, uniting artists and writers. Since that time
they have played Havel's *"Temptation"* and *"Largo Desolato"*, and it seems likely that a plaque will be placed at the
theatre commemorating Havel's employment there in the
1960's, first as a lighting assistant and then as a developing playwright, at the place his plays were first performed before becoming world renowned.

## ■ DIVADLO ZA BRANOU
## – THEATRE BEHIND THE GATE ■

*Otomar Krejča*

Divadlo Za branou, or Theatre Behind the Gate, was opened by the
famous director Otomar Krejča
(b. 1921), on November 23, 1965,
with the performances "Mascara de
Ostende" and "Cat on the Railroad
Tracks", written by Michel de
Ghelderode and Josef Topol,
respectively. The theatre was opened in a hall of Adria Palace, a unique **art deco** building on Národní
Street, which it shared with the theatre **Laterna Magica**.
Divadlo Za branou was closed for political reasons in 1972.

A leading actor and director at the **National Theatre**,
Krejča's new theatre attracted many well known Czech
playwrights, dramaturges, and actors such as Josef Topol,
Karel Kraus, M. Tomášová, J. Tříska, and M. Nedbal, as
well as **philosophers** (Jan Patočka, Josef Šafařík) and stage designer Josef Svoboda. Some of his more famous productions were Chekhov's *"Three Sisters"*, *"Ivanov"* and
*"The Seagull"*, Nestroy, Kraus and Mahler's *"The String*

*with One End"*, de Musset's *"Lorenzaccio"*, Sophocles' *"Oedipus"–"Antigone"*. The performances of the Divadlo Za branou were the jewel of numerous international festivals including: BITEF Belgrade, Théatre des Nations Paris, and World Theatre Season, London.

After his theatre was closed, Krejča went abroad and worked in Brussels and Stockholm, becoming an artistic director at Schauspielhaus in Düsseldorf, and in Paris and Vienna. In 1990 he returned to Prague and re-established the theatre, playing Chekhov's *"Cherry Orchard"* and utilizing dramaturgical methods of the 1960's. He also produced newer productions such as *"Waiting for Godot"*.

## ■ DON GIOVANNI ■

The opera of operas, Don Giovanni, by the composer <u>W.A. Mozart</u> and librettist Lorenzo da Ponte, may be the most famous work ever premiered on a Prague stage. The premiere, which had been postponed several times, was performed on October 29, 1787, at <u>Stavovské–Estates Theatre</u>, conducted by the composer himself. The opera was commissioned by the City of Prague, and Mozart tailored it to Prague audiences, finishing the score at <u>Bertramka</u> villa in Prague 5–Smíchov. The opening was a tremendous success and it quickly gained fame on stages worldwide.

Don Giovanni soon became an integral part of the city itself. After Mozart and director D. Guardasoni, numerous important personages have been at the helm of Don Giovanni as conductors and directors. Three stages, the Stavovské Theatre (historically having the most adequate interior), the <u>National Theatre</u> near the Vltava River, and the current <u>State Opera</u> House (formerly Neues Deutsches Theatre), have traditionally performed the opera, each with its unique installations and interpretations.

In June, 1991, when Stavovské Theatre was under renovation, Prague's first Mozart Open theatre <u>festival</u> featured a study of Don Giovanni, conceived and directed by Karel

Brožek, and performed at the National Marionette Theatre's stage. Brožek's version became a big hit as well, and by 1994 had been performed 700 times! The Marionette Stage is located at No. 1 Žatecká, Prague 1. The highly acclaimed performance attracted great attention: a classic opera title, presented in the magical kingdom of puppets with tasteful humour and lightness, containing a Mozartesque charm and style, it is a hilarious and striking performance. So Don Giovanni continues to live at both Stavovské Theatre and at the unique marionette miniature theatre, enjoying enthusiastic audience responses just as it did when first performed over two hundred years ago.

## ■ ANTONÍN DVOŘÁK ■

Antonín Dvořák (1841–1904) is a Czech composer revered around the world for his refreshing, optimistic and energetic music, and music fans everywhere love the sunny vitality and exciting temperament of his melodies. Prague is intimately linked to his music and five of his popular waltzes are called *"Prague's Waltzes"*. He was hugely popular in the period after **Mozart** and before Janáček and Martinů.

Mozart's work was highly respected by Dvořák, who called him "a little sun" that smiled at the people. Dvořák learnt from Mozart's music, and particularly enjoyed **Don Giovanni,** saying "I love that opera: the depth of the ending is incredibly vast." Dvořák, who was also a conductor and lecturer, visited and gained popularity in England and the United States, and wrote *"The New World"*, a famous symphony included in the repertoire of many of the world's orchestras. He was particularly celebrated and loved in his hometown of Prague. A **baroque**–style villa named "America" was constructed by the renowned architect Kylián Ignác Dienzenhofer at No. 2 Ke Karlovu, Praha 2, which houses the Dvořák Museum. Dvořák lived on nearby Žitná Street for many years so the location of the small country manor is fitting.

## ■ ALBERT EINSTEIN ■

The physicist Albert Einstein (1879–1955), contributed to human culture not only with his research in theoretical physics and the famous *"Theory of Relativity"* but also with philosophical essays and socio–political activity against fascism, militarism and nuclear proliferation.

From 1910–11 he was employed in Prague at the German university as a Professor of Theoretical Physics. He lived at 1215/7 Lesnická Street, Praha 5–Smíchov, (situated on the riverfront between Jirásek and Palacký bridges), which is now designated with a commemorative plaque. From his correspondence, it is clear he enjoyed his time in Prague. Einstein also stayed at 1597/7 Viničná Street, Praha 2–Nové Město, his former institute, which is also commemorated with an honorary plaque.

## ■ THE ESTATES THEATRE – STAVOVSKÉ DIVADLO ■

The Stavovské Theatre was built for Count Nostic in 1781–3, in <u>Classicist</u>-style, and was originally called the Count Nostic Theatre. The nearby <u>Carolinum</u> authorities objected to its proposed location in the small Fruit Market space, because they felt the theatre's proximity was inappropriately close to their complex.

The first performance was Lessing's play *Emilia Galotti* on April 21, 1783. It remained a German theatre until 1799 when it was purchased by The Czech Estates (Estates Theatre). Between 1813 and 1816 the director of the theatre was the great composer <u>C.M. Weber</u>. The Czech State song *"Kde Domov Můj"* was first performed here in

1834. The German–speaking Deutsches Landestheater was re-established in 1862 (when the Czechs moved to the Temporary Theatre that later became the <u>National Theatre</u>), and continued here until 1920 when they were evicted.

After 1920 the Stavovské Theatre became the second stage of the National Theatre and remains so today. Performances are orientated toward classic theatre and they have a modern repertoire: Ionesco, Coltes, Miller, Havel, Topol, and Tabori, and present operas, mostly <u>Mozart</u>. Mozart operas *The Marriage of Figaro* (1787), the premier of <u>Don Giovanni</u> (1787), and *La Clemenza di Tito* (written at the time of King Leopold II's coronation in 1791) were performed at Stavovské, making it one of the more famous buildings in Prague. In the summer months it hosts the chamber <u>Opera Mozart</u>.

## ■ EXHIBITION GROUNDS (VÝSTAVIŠTĚ) ■

In the 1890's several large agricultural and cultural exhibitions were held in the spirit of Czech liberal capitalism. The largest and most important was the Jubilee of 1891, organized to commemorate the 100th anniversary of Prague's Industrial Exhibition of 1791. In 1890–1, on the east of the former Royal Deer Park (known today as Stromovka Park), a large exhibition ground and Industrial Palace was built according to a design by František Prášil and Bedřich Munzberger, with nearby smaller pavilions by Antonín Wiehl. The conception of the areal followed large London and Paris exhibitions of the nineteenth century.

In addition to the still–operational exhibition complex and its unique entrance at U Sjezdového Paláce Street, other tourist attractions such as the funicular railway, The "Eiffel" view tower, the House of Mirrors, all on <u>Petřín Hill</u>, the Merry–Go–Round in front of the Technical Museum on Kostelní Street, and the Hanavský Pavilion on the west end of Letná Plain, were built concurrently for the Jubilee.

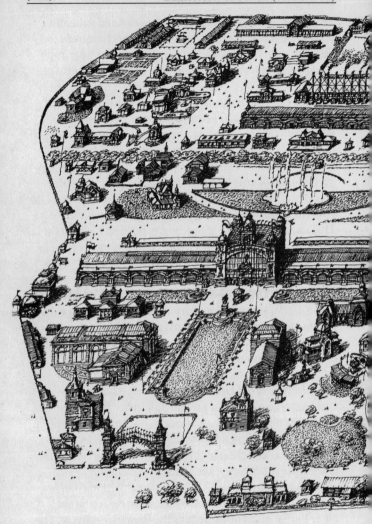

The areal at Stromovka Park was added to in later
exhibitions throughout the years, for example: in 1898,
the circular exhibition depicting the Battle at Lipany
of 1434, painted by Czech naturalist Luděk Marold
(1865–98); in 1960, the Czechoslovak Pavilion by Cubr,

*Exhibition Grounds (1891)*

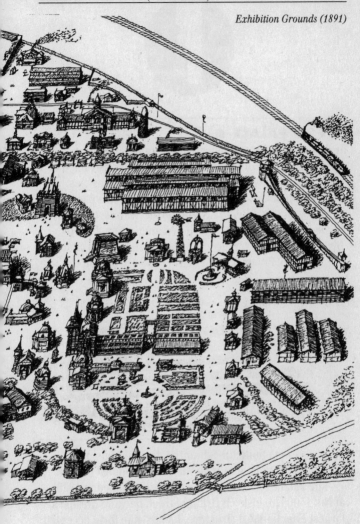

Hrubý and Pokorný from the Brussels Expo of 1958; and,
for the exhibition of 1991, the Pavilion Pyramida, Pavilion
at Křižík's Fountain and the Theatre Spiral (from the original panorama cinema theatre) were built.

## ■ FAIR PALACE ■

In 1918, when Prague became the capital of the Czechoslovak Republic, many buildings were constructed in
the years directly following (that included ministries,
schools, banks, and other public buildings), utilizing Old
Classic and eye–catching Nationalistic architectural styles
incorporating elements Czech ornamentation and <u>cu-
bism</u>. This trend changed however in 1924 when Oldřich
Tyl (1884–1939) and Josef Fuchs (1894–1978) won the

*Fair Palace (1925–28)*

commission to build the administrative and business
building of Sample Fair with their Functionalist design.

The Palace of Prague's Sample Fair, finished in 1928,
at No. 1500 Dukelských Hrdinů Street, became Europe's
largest Functionalist structure. Its box–like form accented
with long slender windows attracted many avant–garde
architects to Prague. Le Corbusier, although intrigued,
after studying it thoroughly in 1928 remarked "a very
important building which after all is not refined enough
to be called architecture."

The original building burned in 1974. It is being re-constructed, in 1994, per the plan of Miroslav Masák and the association SIAL, for use by the **National Gallery** for exhibition of the twentieth century.

## ■ FAUST HOUSE ■

During the time of **Charles the Fourth**, when the New Town was being established, the Counts of Opava constructed what is now known as the Faust House, an historical building located at No. 502 Mladotovský Palace on Karlovo náměstí (Charles Square). Originally rebuilt in the **Renaissance** style, its **baroque** facade was added in the 16th century when it was remodelled for the doctor of Emperor Ferdinand I, Jan Kop of Raumental. The mysterious legend surrounding the house probably began with its previous owner, Count Václav Opavský, an active occultist. Count Opavský's ownership preceded a number of doctors and alchemists who later owned the house, including the infamous English alchemist and charlatan of the Court of **Rudolph II**, Edward Kelley (1590), and by

*Faust House*

the alchemist Ferdinand Antonín Mladota of Solopysky.

The name Faust House comes from Goethe's poem, which relates a variant of the legend, about a Doctor Faust who is taken up by the devil through a hole in the ceiling. Another variation has a young student selling his soul to the devil for gold coins and being taken through the ceiling. It is reputed that the bloodspattered hole defies repair. Between 1833–92, the Faust House was occupied by an institute for deaf mutes. It is currently used as a medical building.

## ■ FESTIVALS ■

Without a doubt the most important cultural festival is Prague Spring, established in 1946. Traditionally it begins on May 12th with a performance of **Smetana**'s *"My Fatherland"* and ends on June 4th with **Beethoven**'s *"9th Symphony d Moll"*. It is organized in Prague's famous concert halls such as the Rudolfinum and **Obecní Dům** (**Municipal House**), and the **Czech Philharmonic** typically participates.

Prague ranks only behind Salzburg and Vienna as the city most associated with **Mozart**'s life. Thus it is appropriate that a new theatre festival, opened in 1991, be named the Mozart Open. The summer festival utilizes specialized stages to present chamber opera and puppet theatre and so on, for internationally accessible performances. It concentrates on classic Mozart as well as new interpretive presentations (for example, **Don Giovanni** by the National Theatre of Marionettes). It also projects the current values of the Czech theatre in work by famous directors from various generations including J. Krofta, J. Schmid, K. Brožek, the Caban brothers, P. Lébl, J. Nekvasil, N. Vangeli, and others.

Another important international festival, the Prague Quadrennial, is held every four years (the latest being in 1991). Exhibitions of scenography and theatre architecture are judged by the Prague Theatre Institute and the winner is awarded the Golden Triga. An international television festival called Golden Prague is held annually by Czech Television.

## ■ MILOŠ FORMAN ■

Miloš Forman is probably the most world famous of all Czech film directors. He was born in Čáslav in 1932 and studied at the Prague Film Academy (FAMU). His early movies – *"Casting Call"* (1963), *"Black Peter"* (1963), *"The Loves of One Blond"* (1965), captivated Czech audiences, and they particpated in the "new wave of Czech film in the 1960's with the advent of co–production."

After the suppression of **Prague Spring**, Forman emigrated to the United States where he has done his best work, including *"Taking Off"* (1971), *"One Who Flew Over the Cuckoo's Nest"* (1975, for which he won an Academy Award for Best Movie), the musical *"Hair"* (1979), *"Ragtime"* (1981) from the novel by E.L. Doctorow, and *"Amadeus"* (1984) which is probably his best known movie, another Academy Award winner, based on Peter Shaffer's play.

*Václav Havel and Miloš Forman*

F

Various scenes in *"Amadeus"* were filmed in Prague. The first scenes were shot at the Invalidovna House in Karlín, the courting scenes in the Rytířský sál at the **Wallenstein Palace** and at the Archbishop's Palace on Hradčanské náměstí, the theatrical scenes at **Stavovské Theatre** (**Estates Theatre**), and the final scenes were filmed at the house of writer Jiří Mucha, son of the well known artist **Alfons Mucha**, in Hradčany.

It should be noted in general, that the Czech film tradition is one of the oldest in the world; the first experimental films and home production were begun at the end of the last century. Rapid expansion of the industry occurred in the 1930's and 1940's when the **Barrandov** Studios were being established. Gustav Machatý contributed to film development by directing classic erotic dramas such as *"Erotikon"* (1929) based upon the work of the **surrealist** poet Vítězslav Nezval, and *"Extase"* (1933), reflected on by Henry Miller in his book *"Max and the White Phagocites"* (besides generating scandal it won a prize at the Venice film festival of 1934). In the 1960's, there was another strong surge of Czech filmmakers, which included Forman, J. Herz, V. Chytilová, E. Krumbachová, J. Jireš, J. Menzel, J. Němec, I. Passer, E. Schorm, F. Vláčil, and others.

*Forman's Amadeus (1984)*

# ■ GARDENS AND PARKS ■

In addition to the gardens and parks of Prague's castles and palaces, there are enough green oases elsewhere in the golden city to fill an entire book describing them all. Since the Middle Ages gardens and vineyards, and later parks, have been popular in Prague.

The earliest gardens were mostly established by the monasteries (<u>Strahov Monastery</u> Gardens, and František's Garden, between <u>Wenceslas</u> and Jungmann <u>Squares</u>). In the <u>Renaissance</u> times gardens were also established at the <u>Prague Castle</u>, located north of the summer chateau Belvedere and surrounded by the Ballcourts House, the Orangeries and the Lions Courtyard (where real lions once roamed), and another Renaissance garden was laid out at the Chateau Hvězda (Star Huntig Lodge).

<u>Baroque</u> gardens are the jewels of many palaces, for example, the <u>Wallenstein Palace</u> on Malá Strana, and there are Baroque terrace gardens southerly of Prague Castle. Beautiful sala terrenas, colonades, grottoes, aviarys, arbors, greenhouses, cascades, pools, fountains, vases, and sculptures are found in the pretty gardens of Wallenstein, Ledeburk, Palffy, Kolowrat and Fürstenberk Palaces. Rich Baroque gardens of this type may also be visited at Vrtbovská Garden (with its beautiful gallery of statues) at the base of <u>Petřín Hill</u>, at Schönborn Palace (presently the US Embassy garden), at Lobkovicz Palace (German Embassy garden), at the garden of Černínský Palace, and at the excellent garden of <u>Troja Chateau</u>, located at the northerly end of the city.

French and Italian architectural styles at the end of the

18th century were modified by the first English–style pub-
lic parks. Prague's first public park was Chotkovy Sady,
below Belvedere Chateau, which is still open. Beautiful
and romantic green oases of Prague can be explored at
Petřínské Sady, at Kampa, at Vojanovy Sady, at Letenské
Sady, the King's Deer Park (or Stromovka Park), at
Riegerovy Sady in Vinohrady, at the garden of Gröbe's
Villa, with its beautiful outdoor theatre, grottoes, casca-
des, and also on the islands of the Vltava River such as
Střelecký and Žofín. The fabulous Botanical Gardens of
Charles University with its tropical, subtropical and desert
greenhouses are located at No. 18 Na Slupi, Nové Město,
and the new botanical gardens near Troja Zoo, built in
1968 on 130 hectares.

## ■ THE GHETTO ■

The remains of the former Jewish ghetto, in the quarter
called Josefov named after King Josef II, are located
between Pařížská and Kaprova Streets and the waterfront.
This area from the time of the Middle Ages was a flou-
rishing district where many Jews resided, worked and
worshipped, and it was rich with mystery and legend.
Between 1893 and 1917 major renovations occurred here
that largely resulted in its "sanitization".

The Jewish culture has been present in the Czech
lands since the ninth century and experienced both favou-
rable and very hard times here. Perhaps the most
sympathetic period was during the reign of the Přemysl
family, during the reign of **Rudolph II**, and during the rule of Josef II, when the wealthy Jews were allowed to move outside the ghetto. From the second half of the 19th
century the Jews could freely move through the city and
the ghetto became a slum for criminals and sin, and mainly poor people lived there. The ghetto was not allowed to
expand laterally so it grew upward and any spare spaces
were filled with housing, giving it an oddly picturesque
look. Transportation and hygiene suffered and debates ra-

ged on whether or not to demolish and rebuild the ghetto (like Hausmann did in Paris) or to leave it intact with its spirit and romance. The latter argument, put forward by the artists of the day, saved areas along Karlova Street and even in Malá Strana from being razed. The ghetto represented a symbol of persecution, and it provided fertile ground for romantic legends such as the <u>Golem</u>.

The nature of the former ghetto can be gleaned from old city plans, from photographs, contemporary documents and memories, and the buildings still standing from those days such as the Early <u>Gothic</u> Old–New <u>Synagogue</u>, the Jewish Cemetery, established in the early 15th century and containing 20,000 tombstones including Rabbi Löw's, and the City Hall, with its clock hands that run the opposite way (inspiring a poem by <u>Apollinaire</u>) can be visited. These places still serve to give the Jews strength and hope, which was sorely needed during the middle of the twentieth century. In 1900, <u>Max Brod</u> describes the 25,000 Jews in Prague as being widespread and prosperous. During the <u>Nazi</u> occupation most of the Jews were killed

*Old Jewish Cemetery*

by the Germans. Today, other important Jewish items
include the rich collections of the Jewish State Museum
housed in the Maisel, Klaus and Pinkas Synagogues with
treasures of 153 Jewish communities covering Bohemia
and Moravia, moved when these communities were
destroyed during the Nazi Holocaust.

    The fame of the ghetto is promulgated, not only by its
historical buildings but also by the legacies left by its great
writers, such as **Kafka**, **Brod** and **Kisch**, its religious figures, its financiers and lawyers, such that even today the
flavour of the old ghetto and its history is sought out by
artists and tourists. As one takes a few steps from the Old
Town City Hall down Železná Street and turns the first
street to the right into one of the ghetto's narrow
cobblestone sidestreets, the magical aura of one of Prague's most special districts quickly fills the imagination.

## ■ GOLDEN LANE ■

The Golden Lane (Zlatá Ulička) in the **Prague Castle**
complex is one of the unique sights of Prague: its bizarre
character dates back to **Rudolph II**'s reign, when his
Castle guards and his gold–smiths lived here and the
street was named after the jewellers. The minute colourful houses were originally built alongside the Castle
fortifications when the Jagellons remodelled the Castle at
the end of the 15th century. Above the houses there was
a covered corridor that united the tower defenses. It was
also used for transferring prisoners from the Justice Hall
in the Castle to the jail of Daliborka Tower.

    From the Golden Lane there is an entrance to the lo-
wer portion of Daliborka Tower (the former prison was
named after Dalibor of Kozojedy). Petr Brandl, a famous
**Baroque** painter from Prague, resided in this prison
unable to pay his debts. In the not too recent past the
Golden Lane was an oasis of tranquility and many people
who wished to work uninterrupted lived in this lane, such
as **Franz Kafka**, Vítězslav Nezval, and Otakar Štorch–Ma-

rien. Today most of thin cute little houses have been converted to small souvenir shops.

## ■ GOLEM AND RABBI LÖW ■

Golem is a shapeless mass or artificial human being from
Hebrew folklore which can be endowed with life. The
term "golem" has entered the world's conciousness
through literature and film. In the Bible it represents an
embryo or germ, symbolizing Adam at the time his body
was created before it contained his soul. In the Talmud,
a golem is a person who lacks intelligence and grace. Documents of the 13th century relate the life–giving caba-
listic rituals associated with the golem, later ones purport
that the golem was created by Rabbi Löw, a famous
Jewish religious authority, to protect Prague's Jewish

quarter (Josefov) and contained certain superhuman powers, derived from the same sources as the human soul, which could destroy persecutors and protect the suffering masses.

Rabbi Löw (1512–1609), is celebrated for creating the golem from soil, water, air and fire, and was a philosopher and founder of the Talmud school (presently the Klaus **Synagogue**). He was the most important rabbi of **Ruldolph II**'s court. He was also an expert in the natural sciences and astronomy, and often met with **Tycho de Brahe**. He is buried in the Old Jewish Cemetary and his grave is often visited.

The writings of Gustav Meyrink (1868–1932), which include *"Golem"* an expressionist gem, are a blend of Jewish myth, reality, imagination and the grotesque. He spent 25 years in the Prague **ghetto** and was intimate with its secrets and mystiques. Other books about Golem have been written by Achim von Arnim, E.T.A. Hoffmann, **E.E. Kisch**, and others. Films of the golem have been made by Paul Wegener (1914) and Julien Duvivier (1935). It was also adapted for opera by Hanuš Bartoň for the Opera Furore at the **Palace of Culture** (1992).

## ■ GOTHIC ■

The cradle of Gothic art is in France, where from 1140 to 1144, the Abbot Suger initiated construction of the Benedictine cathedral St. Denis on the outskirts of Paris which became the model for cathedrals throughout central France. The Gothic style penetrated central Europe mainly through the Cistercian Order. The first Gothic work in the Czech lands is the monasterial hospital Na Františku in Prague, commissioned by the Czech saint, **St. Agnes**, in 1233. Gothic's zenith was reached in the Czech lands during the Luxembourgian dynasty by designers such as William of Avignon, who worked at Roudnice on the Elbe under John of Luxembourg (1333), and Matthew of Arras, who started the St. Vitus Cathedral. Central European

Gothic styles last flourished under **Charles IV**, thanks to Peter Parléř, the creator of the patterned vaulted ceiling and unique flame–like window traceries. The traceries became the motif of the late Gothic and expanded from Prague to the Swiss border (Freiburg i. Br.) and to Strasbourg, Germany, in the 15th century.

There are many outstanding late Gothic monuments in Bohemia, including: the Powder Tower (Prašná brána) in Prague and the eastern part of the St. Barbara's Church in Kutná Hora, both by Matthew Rejsek of Prostějov, and the Vladislav Hall (1493) in **Prague Castle** and the five–tiers of St. Barbara Church in Kutná Hora, created by Beneš Rejt of Pístov.

Under Charles IV, European Gothic painting is culminated in works such as the Author of the Altar of Vyšší Brod, Master Theodorik's paintings, and the Author of the Altar of Třeboň, housed in **National Gallery** in St George's Monastery at Prague Castle.

In the Gothic Era, large scale urbanization was initiated by Charles IV and the resulting New Town utilized many Gothic designs, and Prague became the largest town in Europe. Other early Gothic architecture beside the Monastery of St. Agnes, St. Vitus Cathedral, and the Powder Tower, include Gothic gems such as the Old–New **Synagogue** (around 1280), Old Town Hall, Church of Virgin Mary in front of the Týn near Old Town Square, Bethlehem Chapel, dominating the New Town– is the Church of St. Apollinaire, the Church of the Assumption of the Virgin Mary and of Charles the Great at Karlov, the Church of the Virgin Mary, Na Trávníčku Na Slupi, the Church of St. Stephen on Štěpánská Street, the Monastery Na Slovanech (Emauzy), and the New Town Hall itself in Charles Square. The Charles Bridge is also Gothic, and beautiful Gothic details may be admired on the **Carolinum** building, for example, the unique oriel.

# ■ OTTO GUTFREUND ■

Otto Gutfreund (1889–1927) belonged to the first group
of sculptors who attempted to transfer the principles
of <u>Cubist</u> composition into spacial objects and plastics.
A pupil of E.A. Bourdell in Paris (1909–10), he solved problems of form, using fundamental geometric elements and
lessons learnt from Picasso's cubist analyse of shape. This
led him in 1911 to develop sculptural works featuring
classic cubist composition. In 1912, based on cubist principles, he spatially arranged planar objects adhered to
compose Picasso–like collages. He exhibited these works
at a modern art world exposition in Berlin at the Gallery
Der Sturm, in 1913.

In the 1920's, in accordance with European tendencies,
he solved the then–impact of the Antique, aligning his
Classicism–rooted plastics with architectonic works. This
is seen, for example, in the sculptor's decoration of the
frontal part of the <u>art–deco</u> Adria Palace at Národní třída
in Prague (the building housing the <u>Za branou Theatre</u>),
in the relief frieze on the facade of the Legio–bank at
n.1046 Na poříčí Street, and in the plastic insignia of the
sciences, fitted in the gable on the western flank of the
<u>Clementinum</u> building (Platnéřská Street).

The work of Otto Gutfreund is highly respected, in
a number of world exhibitions of European cubism, for its
philosophical solution of the relationship between form
and content of work addressing the progress of civilization. The plastics of Gutfreund, as a primary representative of cubistic sculpture, can be found in numerous world
collections of modern twentieth century art, such as
thePompidou Centre in Paris and the Museum of Modern
Art, New York.

## ■ HABSBURG DYNASTY ■

The Habsburgs are an old dynasty of sovereigns who
obtained the throne of the Roman Empire and the thrones
of the Czech, Hungarian and Spanish Kingdoms, as well as
the Austrian Kaiser's crown. They went on to rule a vast
portion of Europe, the coasts of Africa and the Americas.
The rise of the Habsburgs goes back to the year 1273
when Rudolph I of Habsburg was elected Roman–German
King. After the defeat of Přemysl Otakar II, the Czech king,
the Habsburg's captured Styria and Austria. From the
fourteenth century, they expanded their power to the eastern Alps where they gained a number of territories at the
same time losing Swabian possessions, in parts of Germany, to resistance in the Swiss cantons. Albrecht's son, Ru-
dolf, was the Czech king from 1306–07. In the second half
of the fourteenth century, the Habsburgs split into the
so–called "Albrecht" line (Lower and Upper Austria) and
the "Leopold" line (controlling the remainder). Under
Albrecht II, the Albrecht line obtained a Roman crown,
and for the first time united Austria, Czech and Hungarian
lands (in 1437–57). This line died out with the death of Ladislav Pohrobek in 1457, however.

The Worm Treaty of April 21, 1521, divided the
Habsburgs into separate Spanish and Austrian lines.
In the period from 1516 to 1526, the Habsburgs managed
to acquire a large power base by inheriting the Spanish
Empire, and, moreover, to create a multinational monar-
chy in central Europe.

The Czech lands were influenced particularly by
the Austrian Habsburgs, who ruled Bohemia and Hungary

first by election, in 1526, and later by heritage, obtaining the Roman crown in 1556. From the Spanish Habsburgs, they inherited parts of current Belgium and most of Italy.

The first Habsburg to assume the Czech throne was Ferdinand I. He was born in 1503, in the Spanish town of Alcala de Henarez. Upon entering Czech territory near Jihlava he vowed to safeguard the country's liberties. On February 24, 1527, he was coronated by Bishop of Olomouc, Stanislav Thurza, in Prague. After the coronation he gained important concessions from the Czech states, above all that his son, after coming of age, could be coronated during Ferdinand's own lifetime. So the Czech kingdom was changed definitively, from an elective one to an inherited one. And it remained in Habsburgs' hands until the First World War.

The Austrian Habsburgs' male blood line died out with the death of Charles IV in 1740. Upon pragmatic sanction, all of the Habsburg territories were inherited by his daughter, Maria Theresa, who by marrying the Lotharingian duke, Francis Stephen, founded the Habsburg–Lotharingian dynasty. Her rule brought important administrative, economic and social reforms, which were culminated under her son, Joseph II. He limited the strength of the Roman Catholic Church, abolished monasteries and convents, supported the development of secular schools, and founded manufactories. In 1781, by patent, he emancipated the serfs and allowed for religious tolerance.

With the Austrian Kaiser title the Habsburg–Lotharingian Dynasty ruled from 1804 to 1918, when the throne was lost as a result of the breakup of Austria–Hungary (on November 14, 1918 in the Czech lands, on April 3, 1919 in Austria, and on November 5, 1921, after two failed monarchist coups by Charles I in Hungary). In 1961, the son of the last Habsburg Kaiser, Otto, denounced the Habsburg dynastic claims.

# ■ JAROSLAV HAŠEK ■

A very popular and prolific Czech humorist, writer and journalist, Jaroslav Hašek wrote over five hundred humorous essays, sketches, poems, and newspaper articles. He is most famous, however, for his book *"The Good Soldier Schweik"* which has been translated into forty languages and sold millions of copies.

Hašek was born on April 30, 1883, and his family house is located at No. 1325 Školská Street, Praha 1– Nové Město, near **Wenceslas Square**. Hašek's father taught at a school on Mikulandská Street and Hašek attended the gymnasium on Žitná Street. He also studied at the Academy of Business on Resslova Street, and apprenticed at Kokoška's Drugstore on Perštýn. In his lifetime, he lived in at least 32 different places in Prague!

Hašek was renowned for his bohemian lifestyle and for his extensive knowledge of Prague's pubs. Hašek, and his hero Schweik, were intimately associated with the pub U Kalicha (At the Chalise, located at No. 14 Na Bojišti) which they made world famous. Another character of the book, a gardener named Josef Kalenda, one day visits all the pubs of Prague on his way to work, beginning with the pub Na Zastávce (On the Stop) and ending with U Krále Brabantského (At the King's Brabant). Hašek died in 1923.

# ■ VÁCLAV HAVEL ■

Playwright, writer, human rights activist, dissident, President of Czechoslovakia (CSFR), and President of the Czech Republic, Havel was born October 5, 1936, in Prague. He learned how to practise as a chemical laboratory technician, he attended night school at the gymnasium, and also studied at the Economic Faculty of the Czech Technical University for two years. He was not admitted to the Film School of the Academy of Performing Arts (FAMU) for political reasons.

After mandatory military service between 1957 and 1959, he began working as a stage hand at ABC Theatre.

After 1960, he worked as lighting technician, dramaturge, and assistant director at **Divadlo Na Zábradlí** (Theatre on the Balustrade). He simultaneously studied dramaturgy at the Theatre Department of the Academy of Performing Arts (DAMU). In the 1960's, he was a member of the Czech PEN Club Centre, chairman of the Circle of Independent Writers, and chairman of the editorial board of the monthly Tvář.

After the occupation in August, 1968, he was forbidden to participate in public and artistic life. He then worked as a common labourer in the Trutnov brewery. He became a founder of the underground, typed Expedice publications of forbidden literary works. In January, 1977, he was a founder of Charter 77 and its first spokesman. On October 18, 1977, he was sentenced to fourteen months in jail, reduced to three years probation, for attempting to damage interests of the Republic abroad. In 1978 and again in 1979, he was detained for subversive activities. In 1979, he was sentenced to four and a half years in jail. He served time until February 7, 1983.

In 1988, he was a member of the Czechoslovak–Helsinki Committee. In 1989, he was accused of inciting against and obstructing justice. He was sentenced to nine months in jail, but was released early, on May 17, 1989, with eighteen months probation. In the same year he served on the board of the Czech PEN Club Centre.

After the **velvet revolution** in 1989, he became a representative of the Civic Forum, and until April, 1990, was the chairman of the Community of Writers. On December 29, 1989, he was elected the first and last President of the Czech and Slovak Federative Republic (CSFR). After its breakup he was elected the first President of the Czech Republic.

In 1964 he married Olga Šplíchalová and they have no children. For many years they have lived in Havel's family home at Jirásek Bridge located at No. 78 Rašínovo nábřeží. In 1993, he moved to his own villa near Prague Castle. His official residence, besides the **Prague Castle**, is the Chateau Lány, west of Prague. A list of his plays include: *"The Garden Party"* (1963), *"The Memorandum"* (1965), *"The Inreased Difficulty of Concentration"* (1968), *"The Beggars Opera"* (1972), *"Audience"* (1975), *"Protest"* (1978), *"Largo Desolato"* (1984), *"Temptation"* (1985) etc.

In addition to his plays, he has also written a number of books, essays, and television and radio plays.

## ■ VÁCLAV HOLLAR ■

Václav Hollar (1607–77) is one of the influential graphic designers in art history. Although he began his artistic career here when he was twenty, Hollar left Prague, not because he was being oppressed as a Catholic, but to seek a wider expression of his talents. He first worked in Mathias Merian's famous graphics laboratory in Frankfurt, where he learned the technique of etching. He later rendered all his work utilizing this method. From 1628 he worked in Strasbourg, for publisher Jacob Van Den Heyden, and between 1630–36 he worked in Cologne. He was then hired by Thomas Howard Arundel, envoy to the English King, producing a series of graphic works of various European towns. In 1636, he visited Prague and from copious notes produced a detailed depiction of Prague that included numerous explanatory notes seemingly tailored for Czech immigrants.

Hollar was renowned for his graphic series', particularly *"Theatrum Mulierum"*, and his poetic folios of shells, butterflies, insects, and women's feather muffs. He also reproduced famous artworks for Arundel while in London. The largest collections of Hollar are at the British Museum, the King's Collection at Windsor, and at the Prague **National Gallery**.

It is interesting that original graphic works of Hollar may still be found in Prague's **antikvariats**. The community of Czech graphic artists have promoted their art in Hollar's name by establishing Association of Czech graphic artists, Hollar in 1917, which has its gallery at No. 6 Smetanovo Nábřeží near the **National Theatre**.

## ■ BOHUMIL HRABAL ■

After **Franz Kafka**, **Hašek**, Kundera, and **Václav Havel** there are not too many internationally known Czech writers, however, Bohumil Hrabal comes close as one of Prague's greatest writers after World War II.

Hrabal was born in Brno on March 28, 1914, and after his early life spent in small towns (working as a brewery hand, a railway dispatcher, and a miner) he came to Prague in the 1940's, to the suburb of Libeň, and began frequenting small pubs in the centre of town. Before he became a professional writer, Hrabal worked in the 1950's and 60's as a recycling paper–packager and as a stage–hand.

The first printings of his books were destroyed and his prose was published only in peripheral magazines: he saw his first book in print when he was over fifty (these include: *Pábitelé*, *Dance Lessons For the Older and Advanced*, *Closely Watched Trains* –which earned Jiří Menzel an Oscar for the film adaption–, *Postřižiny*, *I Served the King of England*, *Tender Barbarian*, *Solitude Too Noisy*, *Bambino di Praga*, etc.).

Today Hrabal's second home could be considered the pub At The Golden Tiger (U Zlatého Tygra) on Husova Street where he spends every evening (except Tuesday and Sunday when for many years he sat in the Krušovice Pub on Široká Street which after its recent renovation he moved in 1993 to the Pub U Hynků on Malá Štupartská Street behind the Týn Church), where he collects impulses and motifs for his work. Hrabal rises early each morning and travels by bus to the village of Kersko where he feeds his cats and writes without breakfast until late

*Bohumil Hrabal and Professor František Dvořák (co–author of this book)*

lunchtime and after lunch goes straight to his pub in Prague to complete the rhythm of his day, leaving around 8 pm for home. Hrabal is faithful to his pub and he has made the U Zlatého Tygra famous, as Schweik did the U Kalicha. The eighty year old writer sits daily with his regular group of people with whom he continues the discussion of literature and the world, a generally exclusive group. An exception to the rule, however, was on November 11, 1994, when he allowed Bill Clinton and Václav Havel to briefly join his club.

## ■ JAN HUS ■

Jan Hus (1371–1415) was undoubttedly one of the most important figures in Czech history. A Rector at Charles University (<u>Carolinum</u>), Jan Hus preached at Bethlehem Chapel in Prague against certain aspects of the Catholic Church. This reformation movement became so powerful in Bohemia that the Council of Constance tried him as a heretic and found him guilty. He was burned at the stake on July 6, 1415.

*The Bethlehem Chapel*

The reforms Hus supported were based upon the ideas of John Wycliffe (1320–84), an English theologian, reformer and bible translator. Hus originally spoke in the Parish Church of Saint Havel in 1404, but his most important and popular sermons were presented in the Bethlehem Chapel on Betlémské náměstí (Bethlehem Square). The Chapel was built in 1391 as a place for religious discourse in the Czech language. It is commonly believed that up to three thousand people attended the Chapel during his sermons (although not all could fit in). The Catholic Church disagreed with Hus' political opinions and the Archbishop banned him from Prague.
A groundswell of support for Hus' teachings, and anger at his execution, eventually led to the Hussite Wars.

In the 18th century the Chapel was demolished and incorporated into houses built over the site. At the time of the First Republic, a decision was made to reconstruct the Chapel. Reconstruction took place between 1948 and 1954, under the supervision of the Prague architect J. Fragner, taking care to imitate the original as closely as possible.

# ■ JAZZ ■

Jazz first came to Prague in 1918, when the first Republic was established. During the World Wars it flourished thanks to such avant–garde artists as theoretician **Karel**

*U.S. President Bill Clinton at the Reduta Jazz Club (January 11, 1994) / Photo by Jiří Jírů*

Teige, and theatre director and musician E. F. Burian, who wrote and published a unique book called *"Jazz"* in 1928. Besides Burian and his theatre group D 34, jazz in Prague gained merit under the composer, conductor and bandmaster of the Osvobozené Theatre orchestra, Jaroslav Ježek. Ježek, along with J. Voskovec and J. Werich, escaped persecution during World War II by escaping to the United States of America, where he died in 1942.

The fascist and **communist** regimes were unfavourable towards jazz music. Since the 1950's, only a handful of jazz clubs existed under the leaderships disapproving eye, such as Reduta, Viola (both on Národní třída) and **Semafor**. Today there are no restrictions on concerts or jazz scores and there are a number of specialized clubs for jazz fans.

The Reduta is still famous; on January 11, 1994, the President of the United States, Bill Clinton, visited the establishment with Czech President Havel and played two songs on a saxophone presented to him by Havel.

Prague's jazz clubs include:
Agharta Jazz Centrum, No. 5 Krakovská,
                    Praha 1–Nové Město.
Euroclub, No. 5 Opletalova, Praha 1–Nové Město.
Malostranská beseda, No. 21 Malostranské náměstí,
                    Praha 1–Malá Strana.
Reduta Jazz Club, No. 20 Národní, Praha 1–Nové Město
Viola Jazz Club, No. 7 Národní, Praha 1–Nové Město

# ■ MILENA JESENSKÁ ■

Milena Jesenská was a left–oriented journalist and Czech translator who became known for her friendship with Franz Kafka, which found literary expression in Kafka's *"Letters to Milena."* Two days after Kafka's death she wrote his obituary in the newspaper Narodní Listy, discussing the substance of his work.

Jesenská was born in Prague, in 1896, and began her career in journalism in Vienna. Originally a **communist**, she left the Party, in 1934, at the time of the government trials and began to criticize communist and fascist ideologies.

She lived a bohemian lifestyle and rumours abound about her relationships with Kafka and avant–garde artists of the interwar period. She was addicted to drugs and spent some time in sanatoriums. Her views were published until the **Nazi** occupation; she worked illegally during the occupation and was eventually arrested, and she died in Ravensbrück on May 17, 1944.

Although somewhat neglected, Jesenská's journalism and progressive views point out certain ideals of the modern Czech woman of this period.

## ■ THE JESUITS ■

The Order of Jesuits, the Society of Jesus (Societas Jesu), was founded by the Spanish noble, Ignacio of Loyola, upon the Papal Bull of Pope Paul III. The Papal Bull, called *"Of the Establishment For the Society of Jesus"*, was issued in 1540. After some months, the members of the Society elected Ignacio their first general and took monastic vows at his hands. The introduction to the monastic constitutions authored by Ignacio states "The goal of this Society is to care by grace of God, not only for the salvation and perfection of one's own soul, but to very actively participate in the salvation and perfection of our neighbours' souls as well."

The Society of Jesus has become one of the more significant elements of the Catholic Church in recent ages. Its main European mission was Catholic renewal as suggested by the Trident council.

In April, 1556, led by German provincial Peter Canisius, the first twelve members of the Society arrived at the Monastery of San Clemente in Prague, on Karlova Street. The role of the Jesuits in the period of re–Catholicization of the Czech lands has been greatly criticized during periods of Czech patriotism, and its reassessment seems imminent.

Important Jesuit figures are closely linked with **Baroque** art, such as Bohuslav Balvín, Bedřich Bridel, and so on.

In 1773 the Pope, under the urging of European governments and the Freemasons, disbanded the Society

*Statue of Ignacio of Loyola*

of Jesus. It was resumed, however, in 1814, and has become the largest male religious order with 27,000 members.
The Jesuits returned to Bohemia in 1853, to San Ignacio
Church in Prague. In 1919, the Czechoslovak viceprovince
was established which included additional communities
such as Silesian.

From 1918 to 1939, and during a short period after
1945, the Jesuits administered several high schools, such
as the Archbishop's Gymnasium in Prague certain places
of pilgrimage, for example, Velehrad and Hostýn, and were active in the Catholic press.

In 1950, like members of other orders, they were
forced into "concentration monasteries". After the **Velvet
revolution** in 1989, their activities were made legal; their
new headquarters is No. 2 Ječná Street, Prague 2.

In the 17th and 18th centuries, the Jesuits erected
magnificant constructions in Prague, for example the
Church and College of San Ignacio at Charles Square,
St. Nicholas at Malostranské náměstí, and the university
complex of the **Clementinum**. The first place the Jesuits
became active was at the Clementinum, near the Charles
Bridge, settling at the same time at the centre of the New
Town. Other important Jesuit buildings include: the
Church of San Salvador at Křížovnické náměstí near Charles Bridge, and the Convict established in a former housing complex and courtyard enclosed by Bartolomějská
and Konviktská streets. The Convict facility served as
a high school dormitory until the order was disbanded
in 1773.

Prague's Jesuit buildings were built by many renowned
architects and designers, such as the famous Carlo
Lurago.

## ■ ST. JOHN OF NEPOMUK ■

St. John of Nepomuk (1350–93) was a very important
Czech religious figure. He studied law in Prague and in
Padua, Italy, and was ordained as a priest in 1380. In 1389

he was promoted to General Vicar, and also became confessor to King Wencelas IV's wife. Nepomuc was arrested because he sought to confirm an abbot of Kladruby Monastery against the king's desires, however, another underlying reason was his refusal to reveal the Queen's confession. In 1393, after being tortured, he was thrown by King Wencelas IV from the Charles Bridge into the Vltava River where he was drowned.

In 1683 his statue was erected on the Charles Bridge and the point from which he was thrown into the river was marked, and in 1727 Nepomuc gained sainthood and became the patron of the Czechs. Saint John of Nepomuk is traditionally known as a defender of personal honour and of the unfairly accused, and also as a guardian of swimmers. For a long time he was the patron saint of the **Jesuits**. He is commonly depicted with a wreath about his head, which contains five stars.

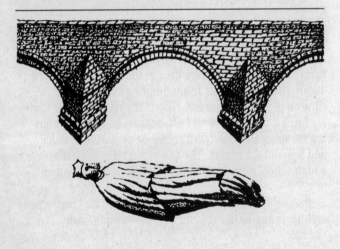

## ■ FRANZ KAFKA ■

The name Franz Kafka represents for many, a magical literary figure of the twentieth century. He was very closely linked with Prague, indeed, he was born there on the July 3, 1883, and only left Prague for short periods of time during his life.

Few authors have influenced modern literature the way Kafka has. He was not an overly prolific author (among his most important books and stories are *America*, *The Metamorphosis*, *The Trial*, *The Castle*), however, a phenomenal bulk of criticism and philosophies have grown up over the century concerning his life and work.

In October, 1907, a year after Kafka graduated, he began working at Assicurazioni Generali on <u>Wenceslas Square</u> and, in August, 1908, he started as a lawyer at the Workers Accident Insurance Company For the Czech Kingdom, at No. 7 Na Poříčí, where he remained until he resigned in 1922 due to an illness (tuberculosis).

Kafka had two careers: he was a clerk and he was an author. At the time of his death he requested of his friend <u>Max Brod</u> that he should destroy his creative writing, which was largely unpublished. One Kafka expert states that "before the First World War, Prague had a particular cultural and social atmosphere and it heralded the doom of an epoch of European culture, its psychic and philosophical elements, this being personified within the fra-

mework of Prague's German enclave and Jewish **ghetto**. The genius of Kafka is in his expressive motifs of power and absurd bureaucracy and the resultant feelings of danger which marked the fate of mankind for the long–term. After the Second World War Kafka's work, then, instead of falling into oblivion, rose from the ashes as a dramatic testimony, a mysterious phantom emerging from the depths of history."

If we follow Franz Kafka's life, we discover his former family house on the corner of Maiselova and U Radnice Streets near the Old Town Square at the former ghetto is now a Kafka exhibition space ( and, not far away, near the Old Town Square at the corner of Pařížská is the Oppel House where Kafka lived and wrote his famous *"The Metamorphosis"*, in 1913–4).

Young Kafka studied at the German gymnasium in the Kinský Palace in the Old Town Square (on the righthand corner of that building Kafka's father, Hermann, owned a haberdashery). Kafka's family lived in the Sixtus House at No. 2 Celetná from 1888–9, in the beautiful **Renaissance** House "U Minuty" near Old Town Square from 1889–96, and in No.3 Celetná in the corner of Týn's Church from 1896–1907, when he graduated at the historical **Carolinum**. He first practiced law in the House of Justice, located near Fruit Market. In the years of the First World War, from 1916–7, Kafka lived on the **Golden Lane** in the **Prague Castle**, then at Schönborn Palace (No. 15 Na Tržišti Street in Malá Strana, presently the US Embassy). His favorite **cafe** was Cafe Arco at No. 16 Hybernská Street. He enjoyed summer bathing in the Vltava River at the **Classicist**–style swimming bath near Čechův bridge, where he kept a cloakroom paid in advance.

Kafka died at the young age of 41 in the village of Kierling on June 11, 1924, and was buried at the New Jewish Cemetery in Olšany (in Prague 3). His tombstone reads Dr. Franz Kafka and is worth visiting.

---

# ■ JOHANNES KEPLER ■

Johannes Kepler (1571–1630), the famous German astronomer, worked in Prague in the 17th century with **Tycho de Brahe**. Kepler promoted the heliocentric theory of planetary movement and discovered three laws of planetary motion around the sun.

Tycho de Brahe requested of Kaiser **Rudolph II's** court that he be allowed to bring the oustanding Kepler to work with him in Prague. At the time, others invited to Rudolph II's court included G. Bruno, Brahe himself, Tadeáš Hájek of Hájek, the famous doctor Jan Jessinus, and

*Johannes Kepler*

others, all outstanding scientists and alchemists of the day.

In Prague Kepler lived at No. 573/12 Ovocný Trh, with the important Czech astronomer and Charles University professor Martin Bacháček of Naumĕřice. From 1608–12, Kepler lived at No. 188 Karlova Street during which time he discovered two important physical laws regarding planetary movement around the sun. This house displays a commerative plaque and there is a bust of Kepler in the courtyard.

## ■ EGON ERWIN KISCH ■

Perhaps Prague's most famous German writer and journalist, Egon Erwin Kisch (1885–1948), was known as the "Furious Reporter" after his book of the same name published in 1928. The book cover characterizes him accurately: "... one of the most adventuresome of our time, E.E. Kisch has worked as a deepsea diver, once spent the night in the Apache district of London's Whitechapel, was present when the viennese criminal Breitwieser was shot, escaped during the war by plane over Venice, lived in Constantinople, was tatooed, sailed from Prague to Hamburg on the Vltava steamer *A. Lanna 6*, accompanied Slovak emigrants on their journey to France, survived submarine warfare, served as watchman at St. Stefan's Tower in Vienna, studied to be a clown in Denmark, worked in a slaughterhouse, associated with business men in the Ruhr, and adventured as a statist in the movie industry."

Kisch was born in the house "At Two Golden Bears" on the corner of Melantrichova and Kožná Streets, near the Old Town Square, where a commemorative plaque has been placed in honour of him. The son of a Jewish textile merchant, he studied engineering at Prague's German Technical School and german studies at Prague's German University, and later studied journalism in Berlin.

He worked for the *Prager Tagblatt* and *Bohemia* newspapers in Prague, and for newspapers in Berlin. During the First World War he had many adventures, ending up with the Red Guards during the Vienna Revolution of 1918. From there he returned to Prague in 1920, where he associated with the likes of **J. Hašek** and avant–gardist extraordinaire Emil Arthur Longen. He worked for Prague newspaper *Lidové noviny* as their Berlin correspondant from 1922–24, then reported from places around the world such as the United States, Soviet Union and China. He was arrested in Berlin after the fire at the "Imperial Assembly" and upon his release became strongly anti–fascist. He participated in the Spanish Civil War, then emigrated to the USA and Mexico, where he joined a German commune. In 1946 he returned to Prague in poor health where he died two years later at No. 22 U Laboratoře, Praha 6–Střešovice.

His work, inspired by a periphery lifestyle, is fascinating and includes: *"Der Mädchenhirt"*, *"Prague Pitaval"*, *"Marktplatz der Sensation"*, and travel diaries: *"Cars, Pops, Bolsheviks"*, *"American Paradise"*, *"Secret China"*, *"Landing in Australia"*, and *"Discoveries in Mexico"*.

# ■ JIŘÍ KOLÁŘ ■

*Jiří Kolář – self-portrait*

Jiří Kolář (b. 1914) emigrated to Paris in 1980, where he now lives, exhibiting at the Maeght Gallery there. In 1979, a retrospective of his work was presented at the Guggenheim in New York, and his monograph was published in Nürnberg (1979) and Milan (1981).

In the early 1940's, Jiří Kolář was a poet affiliated with the artists' of Group 42, whose motif was to "discover the world in which one lives". In the 1960's, he not only fulfilled certain poetic endeavours but pushed them to new limits. He interpreted his poetry through the creation of collages, and made collages which deconstructed and fragmented renowned art works, photographs, and book print. Through these methods he advanced the artistic discipline of collage, providing unique insights on familiar objects and compositions.

Jiří Kolář has had hundreds of exhibitions and is noted in many monographs and magazines. Currently , worldwide, he is probably one of the best known Czech artists, and one of the more progressive and successful artists of the twentieth century.

## ■ LATERNA MAGICA ■

Laterna Magica, or Magic Lantern, is a theatre that focuses on optical experimentation using film, lighting, projections, radiophonic collage, singing, dance, and lively performers. The theatre first appeared at the Brussels Expo of 1958. French film historian, Georges Sadoul, noted that the Laterna Magica was the biggest draw of the Expo and people crowded into the small Czechoslovak pavilion to see the show.

The project's creator was the famous artistic director Alfred Radok (1914–76) who collaborated with Josef Svoboda, the most famous post–war stage designer, who until recently was the also a director of Laterna Magica as well as an architect. Radok also worked with the young filmmaker **Miloš Forman** who wrote scripts.

A combination of film projection and live actors, in performances such as Offenbach's *Hoffmann's Stories*, and *Revue From the Box* became very popular, particularly when it was new. In time, some felt the rapid technological advances and the perfection achieved in execution diminished the spontaneity and creativity of the performances, but the performances remain unique and entertaining. The theatre has travelled abroad many times, for example, New York City and Montreal (Expo '67).

The theatre has moved from Adria Palace (presently restored as **Theatre Behind the Gate II**) to New Stage, affiliated with the **National Theatre**, on **Národní třída** and it sometimes also plays in the **Palace of Culture** which can house up to 3000 people.

## ■ LITTLE JESUS – BAMBINO DI PRAGA ■

Prague's Little Jesus, or Bambino di Praga, is a sacred statue made of wax by a Spanish Master of the 16th century
and donated to the Order of Carmellites. The seventeen
inch high statue currently resides at the Church of Victorious Virgin Mary on Karmelitská Street, Malá Strana, the
first **Baroque** building in Prague (built 1611–13). (Three
famous Baroque paintings by Petr Brandl are also displayed in the church).

The Little Jesus is worshipped in Spain and its cult is
practised in Italy and South America as well. The statue
originated at the time of the breakup of a monastery
between Sevilla and Cordoba. The monk Joseph was
known for his special worship of Little Jesus and the Holy
Family of Nazareth: a child appeared before him with an
invitation to pray then disappeared, what remained was
a longing to see the child's face again and thus the creation of the statue. The monk was not satisfied with its
look, however, the revelation reappeared before him and
the work was finished in his likeness. When the revelation
left him, Joseph, tired but happy, drifted off to sleep fore-
ver. An authentic, consecrated copy was presented to the
City of Sevilla at Expo '92.

The Little Jesus is an example of Spanish influences in
Prague under the **Habsburg dynasty** coming after French
and Italian influences of the Luxembourgian times (see:
**Gothic** and **Renaissance**). The clothes of Little Jesus are
ceremonially changed several times a year.

## ■ ADOLF LOOS ■

A leader in modern European architecture, the Viennese
architect Adolf Loos (1870–1933) was born in the Moravian town of Brno. From the 1900's, he had numerous
Czech clients. He designed apartment complexes as well
as family homes. The first family home he built in Bohemia was the Bauer Villa (1917–18) in Hrušovany near
Brno. Other important homes include the Brummel Villa

*Müller's Villa 1928–30*
*(architect Adolf Loos)*

(1927–29) in Plzeň and the Winternitz Villa (1931–2) in Prague at No. 10 Na Cihlářce.

Perhaps his best known villa in Bohemia, however, was constructed in Prague between 1928 and 1930 for František Müller, a wealthy building contractor. The villa is located at No. 14 Nad Hradním Vodojemem, Praha 6 – Střešovice. Loos, a unique purist, utilized his technique of Raumplan, which does not use conventional floors to divide the living space but a series of cascading spaces and levels inter–connected with short stairways. The villa was fitted with **Rococo** and **Classicism** furniture pieces as well as furniture designed by Loos himself.

After 1948, the villa was occupied by a publishing house and later became a storage site for archives of the Czechoslovak Communist Party. A group of Czech architects intend to refurbish the unique villa and its interiors and open it to the public.

# ■ MÁNES ■

The Mánes Functionalist building is named after a famous Czech painter Josef Mánes who designed the Old Town Astronomical clock. Mánes was built in the 1930's, designed by Otakar Novotný as not only a gallery but a restaurant and **cafe**, on the former location of the 15th century **Renaissance** Šítkovy mills (its tower still stands next to Mánes).

The Mánes artist's group was established in 1898 by Antonín Slavíček, Jan Štursa, Jan Preisler, Max Švabinský, Jan Kotěra, Josef Gočár, Pavel Janák, Bohumil Kubišta, Emil Filla, Václav Špála, Vincenc Beneš, and **Otto Gutfreund**, making it the most progressive gallery in the Czech lands. They also published books and magazines of art, (Free Movements, for example), and other publications. In the 1930's the avant–garde, such as **Teige** and Nezval, also held meetings there, and artists from elsewhere were invited to lecture and exhibit, such as the **surrealists** Paul Eluard and Andre Breton. Mánes organized the first foreign exhibition of Auguste Rodin in 1902, Edvard Munch in 1905, and the first surrealist exhibition called *Poetry 1932*, attended by S. Dali, G. de Chirico, M. Ernst, P. Klee, A. Giacometti, R. Magritte, H. Arp, and the Czechs represented by J. Štyrský, Toyen, J. Šíma, F. Muzika, A. Wachsmann, F. Janoušek, and J. Makovský. In 1936 **Sudek** and Funke established the photographic subsidiary of Mánes and held an International Photography exhibition, attended by H. Bellmer, J. Heartfield, Man Ray, A. Rodčenko.

The Mánes group was ended in 1948 and then

re-established in 1989 as an artistic club that organizes shows and exhibitions. Mánes is the seat of editorial offices of the *Atelier* and *Visual Art* magazines.

## ■ T.G. MASARYK ■

Professor T.G. Masaryk, the first Czechoslovak President, is among the most important **philosophers**, politicians and statesmen whose life was linked to Prague.

Tomáš Garrigue Masaryk was born on March 7, 1850, at Hodonín. He studied at gymnasium in Brno and at university in Vienna, where he was awarded the Doctor of Philosophy degree in 1876. In 1882, after receiving extraordinary academic honours, he was appointed Professor of Philosophy at Charles University which had just then been re-established. He waged literary and political debates, particularly in relation to the authenticity of two manuscripts (the *"Královédvorský"* and *"Zelenohorský"* manuscripts). He protested against the biased judiciary, and after World War I broke out, he initiated resistance abroad against Austria-Hungary, convinced that the demise of the monarchists was imminent.

The Allies definitively recognized the Czechoslovak Resistance and Masaryk's activities in exile, which culminated in the *"Washington Declaration"* of October 18, 1918, declaring an independent Czechoslovak Republic. The new Republic was intended to reflect philosophical and political concepts of an independent state as described in Masaryk's works.

In November, 1918, Masaryk was elected the first President and re-elected in 1920, 1927, and 1934. He rapidly gained an outstanding ethical authority and influence with his tireless support of democracy.

On March 7, 1990, a belated commemorative plaque in Masaryk's honour was unveiled in the Federal Assembly building. In addition, one of the first decisions of President **Havel** was to initiate development of a T.G. Masaryk Institute at the President's Office.

*T. G. Masaryk and Karel Čapek*

Masaryk during his life had contact with outstanding cultural personalities such as Leo Tolstoy and Romain Rolland. He participated in regular Friday meetings of prominent intellectuals and artists held at **Karel Čapek**'s villa.

The primary works of Masaryk include *"Suicide as a Mass Phenomenon of Modern Civilization"*, *"The Czech Question"*, *"Jan Hus"*, *"Karel Havlíček"*, *"Palacký's Idea of the Czech Nation"*, *"Our Current Crisis"*, *"Fighting for Religion"*, *"Russia and Europe"*, *"The Social Question"*, and *"Humanitarian Ideals"*.

The tradition formulated by Masaryk on the idea of democracy served as a guideline during the **velvet revolution** and represented a bulwark to return to after fifty years of **nazism** and **communism**.

Masaryk's political concept resulted from his philosophical and sociological analyses of the spiritual situation of modern man. He emphasized a harmony of reason and compassion and behaviour, he drew from a positivist's line of thinking, from scientific criticism, and from unrevealed religion.

# ■ W.A. MOZART ■

Born in Salzburg on January 27, 1756, a resident of Vienna and a frequent guest of Prague, Wolfgang Amadeus Mozart quickly entered Czech musical history to remain a permanent bulwark of Czech culture. His stardom in Prague, which had not yet extended to Vienna, he secured early on by performances of the operas *"Kidnapped from Serail"* and *"The Wedding of Figaro"*. It was in a large part due to his appreciative audiences in Prague that Mozart became legend almost immediately in Bohemia, particularly after his death in 1791.

Mozart was 35 years old when he died and his departure was a tragedy for the world's music lovers because his genius was without a doubt extraordinary.

Mozart, as a child prodigy, travelled throughout Europe playing the finest instruments at exquisite palace halls, and as he grew older he soon became an integral part of Prague life. He didn't close himself off into a magical world of tunes but walked through the town as though he were a native: he visited aristocratic homes, music salons, as well as the many pubs, where he played billiards, drank coffee, and spoke to the people of Prague. Oftentimes, late at night, he walked from **Stavovské divadlo** (**Estates Theatre**) as far as to **Bertramka** villa, where he enjoyed the hospitality of the Dušek couple. As their houseguest he was pampered and they provided an environment for him to work undisturbed and untroubled.

The first time Mozart visited Prague in January, 1787, he recorded his impressions as follows: "I looked on with pleasure how all the people were filled with joy listening to the music of my Figaro... nobody talks about anything but Figaro here. All of them play, whistle and hum nothing but Figaro. They do not go to any opera but Figaro. It is a great honour for me..." After he conducted *the Wedding of Figaro* on January 20, 1787, and was very much applauded, the composer/conductor stated the now famous words: "My dear Praguers understand me!"

Mozart's second visit to Prague was from August to November, that same year. The genius first stayed at U tří lvíčků (At the Three Little Lions) on Uhelný trh (Coal Market Square) and later at the Dušeks' Villa Bertramka in Smíchov. On October 29, 1787, "**Don Giovanni**", the opera of operas, premiered at the Estates Theatre. His third visit was in April, 1789, and, finally, during his last stay in Prague, the opera *"La Clemenza di Tito"* premiered on September 6, 1791.

According to his companions when Mozart played billiards he sang the latest tunes he was composing in Vienna, which they later identified as the motifs of the quintet of Tamino, Papagano and the Three ladies from the *"Magic Flute"*. As a freemason Mozart had frequented Prague's Masons' Lodge, Zur Wahrheit und Eintracht, where he promised the masons to compose something "higher", ie., the *"Magic Flute"*.

Today we can listen to Mozart's music in Prague at the monumental Estates Theatre and Bertramka Villa, the latter houses the Mozart Museum, and also in a number of theatre and concert halls. His operas are performed by the Opera Ensemble of the **National Theatre** in its Stavovské facility and his music is performed by a very special music ensemble called **Opera Mozart** on Novotného lávka.

*Mozart's Don Giovanni at the National Marionette Theatre*
*– since 1991: more than 700 performances!*

Mozart's work is also performed at the Mozart Open, Prague's Mozart **festival**, held annually since 1991 that concentrates on nonconformist Mozartian activities. *"Don Giovanni"* is also performed in a unique classic mario- nette version at the National Marionette Theatre, which is thus far the most successful Mozart performance of the 1990's in Prague. The ties of Mozart and Prague are also evoked in the film *Amadeus*, directed by Czech emigré **Miloš Forman**.

## ■ ALPHONSE MUCHA ■

Alphonse Mucha (1860–1939) was world renowned as a decorative painter and as a poster artist in Paris in the 1900's, during the La Belle Epoque. As he was one of the most important practitioners of the **secese** style, the mo- vement was also known as Mucha–style. In 1887 after stu- dying at the Munich Academy and working as a theatre set painter and theatre decorator in Vienna, he moved to Pa- ris (1887). At first an illustrator, he soon became famous in Paris by creating posters for the actress Sarah Bernhardt and her theatre.

In 1904 he was welcomed to the United States as the most important decorative painter in Europe, and from that time his residence alternated between the United Sta- tes, where he taught, and Paris.

He moved to Prague in 1910, working on a cycle of paintings called *"Slavic Epopej"*. Mucha's secese style, ho- wever, soon became outdated and was replaced by the de- velopment of new artistic styles, and he became a symbol of outmoded art. In the 1960's there was renewed interest in secese art and Mucha was rehabilitated, and two exhi- bitions, one at the Victoria and Albert Museum in London and the other at the Grosvenor Gallery, secured his place in art history. His work can be seen in Prague at the **Na- tional Gallery** and at the Art and Industry Museum. His interior design skills can also be enjoyed inside **Obecní dům** (**Municipal House** at náměstí Republiky).

# ■ THE NABIS–PROPHETS GROUP ■

The group was first manifested in Paris with an exhibition held at the Volpini Cafe and consolidated by later showings by Maurice Denis, Edouard Vuillard, and particularly Pierre Bonnard and Odilon Redon. They attempted a new synthetic art based on the colourist inventions of impressionists, applying them in a planar sense taking into account narrative subject–active values, particularly inspired by certain ideas of Paul Gauguin which utilize planar colour shapes in the form of decorative stylizations. Moreover, the group's work shared affinities to the music of **Richard Wagner** and Claude Debussy.

The remarkable work of the Parisian Nabis painters is preserved in Prague, especially their early work. They include the entire interior of the pseudo Romanesque Church of Saint Gabriel, on Holečkova Street in Smíchov, with its decorations created by the two Benedictines, Desiderius Lenz and Jan Verkade in 1895–97, who both came to Prague from the centre of the movement in Beuron in Bavaria. Since the 1880's the movement tended toward efforts to associate new artistic forms with Cathedral subjects of the early Middle Ages. Remarkably, it was because Jan Verkade was a member of the Nabis group in Paris, that Prague gained a unique work known as the Sistine Chapel of Prophets. The work is topical today as Nabists, after highly successful exhibitions in Zürich and the Grand Palais in Paris recently, are being considered "the prophets of modern art". The original decoration is thus an extraordinary cultural attraction, however, it is only accessible during Mass.

# ■ NATIONAL GALLERY ■

The origins of this top state institution, designed to conserve and publicly exhibit the arts, go back to the establishment of a private picture gallery by the Society of Patriotic Friends of the Arts in 1796, as conceived by Francis, Count of Sternberg–Manderscheid. In 1811, Sternberg Palace on Hradčanské Square was purchased to house its collections. The gallery became internationally known in 1843 after Dr. Josef Hoser bequeathed his collection of 17th century Dutch paintings to the gallery.

In 1885, the collections were moved to a specially constructed rear wing of the newly built Rudolphinum. After Czechoslovakia was established, however, the gallery was moved again because the Rudolphinum became the House of Parliament.

In 1929, under the supervision of its curator Dr. Vincenc Kramář, who collected the unique **Cubist** paintings that include Picasso, the gallery was installed in the upper rooms of the Municipal Library. The gallery became a state institution in 1937, and, after 1945, the current National Gallery was formed by combining this gallery and the Modern Gallery.

Nowadays the collections of the National Gallery are exhibited in Sternberg Palace at Hradčany (Old and Modern World Arts), at Jiřský klášter (St. George Monastery) behind St. Vitus Cathedral (Old Czech Arts Till the End of the 18th Century), at **St. Agnes Monastery** in the Old Town (Czech Art of the 19th Century), at Kinský Palace at Staroměstské náměstí (Collection of Graphic Art), and at the Chateau Zbraslav near Prague (Czech Sculpture of the 19th and 20th Century).

The collections are housed in very historic buildings, for example, the St. Agnes Monastery is a former convent of Clarists and the first **Gothic** building in the Czech land, while the **Chateau Zbraslav** is the work of the famous **Baroque** architect Santini.

# ■ NATIONAL THEATRE ■

The National Theatre is one of the most important theatres in the Czech Republic. The National Theatre was
a result of the re–emergence of Czech nationalism, after
its defeat in the Battle of 1848, funded in part by public do-
nations. Land adjacent to the Vltava River was purchased

*National Theatre
–section (1883)*

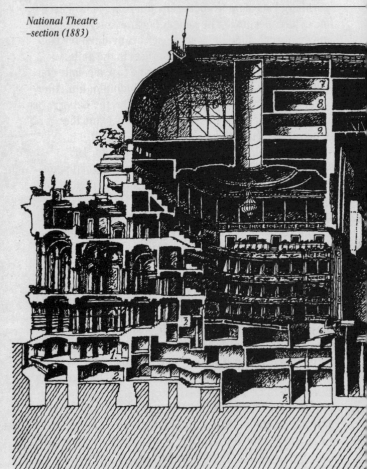

in 1852. In 1862 the Temporary Theatre was built there, now located at the rear portion of the National Theatre building. The foundation stone for the original National Theatre was placed in 1868 and the entire nation celebrated in folk costumes through the streets of Prague. Josef Zítek won the competition to design the theatre and he

worked with Josef Schulz, the designer of the Rudolphinum (the location of Prague Spring and the home of the
**Czech Philharmonic**), the New Colonade in Karlovy Vary,
and the Weimar Museum.

The first National Theatre, designed to seat an audience of 1700 people, was near completion in 1881 when it
caught fire and burned. It was rebuilt per the North Italian
late–Renaissance design of Schulz and opened on November 18, 1883. The first night performance was **Smetana**'s opera *Libuše*, a monumental symbol of national
pride.

The theatre, with its rich ornamentation, represents some of the best architecture of the 19th century in the
Czech lands, and the artists involved were called the generation of the National Theatre (who included the
painter M. Aleš, designer of the foyer, F. Ženíšek, the
creator of the main ceiling, V. Hynais, curtain designer,
and B. Schnirsch and J.V. Myslbek, designed the roof statues).

The National Theatre, nicknamed The Little Golden
Chapel, maintains a high–level of dramaturgy and acting.
The classic theatre is very dynamic, and performs primarily at the National Theatre proper and also at the **Stavovské** (which also plays **Mozart**'s operas) and small experimental Kolowrat Theatre, the latter two theatres being
administered by the National Theatre. The directors are
excellent and include the likes of Ivan Rajmont, Jan Kačer
(from the **Činoherní Klub**), and Miroslav Krobot. The
New Stage of the National Theatre, located next door to
the National Theatre building, is let to **Laterna Magika**.
The Kolowrat Theatre space in the Kolowrat Palace is let
to the National Theatre by the Count of Kolowrat for one
crown per year.

## ■ NAZISM ■

When the Nazis came to power in Germany in 1933 and
Hitler began developing plans to extend the Third Reich,

from the outset Czechoslovakia was among those nations whose sovereignty was threatened. In 1938, Czechoslovakia, in response to Hitler's plans to administer the Sudeten territory, mobilized its citizens twice in defense. However, after the Western powers (France and England) accepted Hitler's Munich plan which supposedly ensured peace in Europe, the Czechoslovak government agreed to give up the Sudeten territory, a move which inflicted irreversible damage to the 20 year old country. In addition to negative political and economic consequences, the country lost its continuous line of defense when it acquiesed to the Nazi expansion.

On March 15, 1939, Hitler's Germany breached all its guarantees and vows to France and England and occupied the remainder of the Czechoslovak state. Slovakia had seceded immediately prior, and as a puppet state fought on the German side until the end of the war.

On March 15, Adolf Hitler journeyed from Česká Lípa via Mělník, through the Kobylisy and Letná districts of Prague and arrived at **Prague Castle**. He stayed in the right wing of the castle, protected by SS units and armoured vehicles. In the afternoon he drove through the streets of Prague and met an assembly of German undergraduates in the first yard of the castle. That night he worked out the declaration for the establishment of the Protectorate of Bohemia and Moravia.

At 11 am on March 16, according to K.H. Frank, Hitler stood at the window of the castle and enjoyed Prague's beauty. Of **Petřín** Tower he said, "That metal contraption has to disappear, it interferes with the grandeur. Something magnificent should be built in its place that symbolizes the town's significance."

So the Protectorate of Bohemia and Moravia was established in the Czech lands, headed by the State President and the Reich Protector. Four men held the post of Reich Protector; among them was Konstantin von Neurath who was sentenced in Nuremberg in 1946 to fifteen years

*March 16, 1939, Adolf Hilter enjoyed Prague's beauty*

in prison. The second person was the top leader of Third
Reich Security, SS Obergruppenfuehrer Reinhard
Heydrich, who was assigned to Prague on September 27,
1941, to suppress the Czech resistance group called "In
the Heart of the Great German Reich". After Heydrich was
assassinated Kurt Daluege was appointed Protector, he
was later sentenced to death by the Czechoslovak People's
Tribunal and executed. The fourth Protector was Wilhelm
Frick who was sentenced in Nuremberg in 1946 and executed. In reality most political matters in the Protectorate
were directed by K.H. Frank, born in Karlovy Vary, who
was State Secretary and later State Minister.

The Czechs became increasingly dissatisfied with the occupation and martial law had to be declared in 1941. In 1942, resistance peaked with the assassination of Heydrich by Czech paratroopers trained in Great Britain. They pitched a bomb into his car, rounding a turn in Hole-šovice, and Heydrich died of his wounds a few days later. His funeral ceremony was in front of Matthews Gate at Prague Castle on June 7, 1942, at 6 pm. As he lay in state Himmler, Daluege and Frank stood nearby.

The assassination initiated a bloody retaliation in the Czech lands: dozens of suspects and their families were murdered, resistance organizations were wiped out, and the village of Lidice near Kladno was razed to the ground (the male inhabitants were all killed, all the women were sent to concentration camps, and their children were sent to German families to be brought up as Nazis). The name Lidice is a symbol of Nazi terror, as is Ležáky, another village that suffered the same treatment several months later.

The Nazi occupation resulted in 300,000 dead, in addition to tens of thousands of Czech Jews who were sent to extermination camps via the Terezín ghetto.

Although only 21,000 Germans resided in Prague at the time of the occupation, the Nazis attempted to transform it back into a German town. It was designated by the Nazis to represent an old German town, a centre of medieval German culture, the location of the oldest German university and so on. Several proposals and schemes were developed in order to reorganize Prague, fortunately however, the Nazis were unable to implement them. In 1939–40 plans for large scale housing projects for high level German officials were developed for the Letenská plain, and for Petřín near the tower for large SS and police armouries. There were also plans to build a German university, a scientific society, and a large research institute for south–eastern Europe.

The main instrument and coordination centre for the

development of a new German Prague was to be the
"Planning Commission for the Capital of Prague and Its
Surroundings", established by the Protectorate government on January 25, 1940, after the former state regu-
lation commission. It's chairman was a Berlin professor,
Niemeyer, who had been recommended by the head
architect of Berlin's construction works, and Hitler's fa-
vourite man, Albert Speer.

Niemeyer's conceptual plans (1940) included the following: numerous monumental buildings on the left bank of
the Vltava River; Nazi governmental administrative offices
near Prague Castle; near Petřín and **Strahov** some public
buildings, congress halls, and facilities for the Nazi party;
some university buildings at Letná; a house of representatives of the City of Prague near the Charles Bridge; and
a new cultural and residential centre for Prague Germans
in **Baba**–Bubny. This new urban zone was to be linked to
the ancient and Theresian German town along the Vltava
River. Other Nazi organizations were to be located at
Kampa and on Střelecký Island. The Czech population
was to be gradually displaced to the right bank.

Niemeyer's concept encountered resistance among
Prague Germans, headed by K.H. Frank, and was eventually discarded. Other concepts were not forthcoming, the
idea was hampered by turns in the war.

The following locations are associated with the Nazis
in Prague: the institution called Arbeitsamt für politische
Propaganda was the Prague office of SS Gruppenführer
K.H. Frank, who later became the State Secretary, when
he worked for the Sudeten German Party at No. 4 Hybernská Street, Prague 1; the office of the Protector, later
moved to Prague Castle, at Černínský Palace on Loretánské Square, Prague 1–Hradčany; a former bank, it was
used for the Gestapo headquarters, at Petschek Palace at
No. 20 Politických vězňů, Prague 1; the villa of K. H. Frank
at No 11 Na zátorce, Praha 6– Bubeneč; the right flank of
the Prague Castle, the residence and offices of the Reich

Protector Reinhard Heydrich; the curve in Kirchmayerova Street where the Mercedes Cabriolet of Reinhard Heydrich was bombed by Czech resistance fighters on May 27, 1942 and nearby Na Bulovce Hospital where Heydrich was treated and died; the Church of Charles Boromejský at Resslova Street, Prague 2, where the seven resistance paratroopers, including the two actual assassins, were cornered in an extensive German manhunt and killed or committed suicide; Hotel Alcron at No. 4 Štěpánská, Prague 1, where in 1944 the Russian General Vlasov who headed the Committee for Setting Free the Nations of Russia (an anti–Stalinist army) stayed, as did Rose–Marie Feil, K.H. Frank's lover, who had a special direct telephone line to Frank.

*Old Town City Hall
– destroyed by Nazis on May, 1945*

# ■ JAN NERUDA ■

Prague of the 19th century is probably best portrayed in the work of the poet Jan Neruda (1834–91). Neruda used typical Prague folk figures in works such as *"Arabesques"*, *"Malostranské Stories"*, and *"Ragamuffins"*. He also described the 1848 revolution in his *"Cemetery Flowers"* and *"Books of Verses"*, and he meditated over the future of man in the poetry collection *"Cosmic Songs"*.

In his newspaper essays he relates the fast-paced life of Prague's marketplace (Uhelný Trh) around Saint Havel's Church, life on the Charles Bridge and along narrow streets around Bethlehem Square (Betlémské náměstí).

In his youth Neruda met his friends in the cafe "Čáslavského" on the corner of Dominikánská and Perštýn Streets, or at "U města Moskvy" on Na Můstku where they established the famous literary group Máj. The poet was deeply interested in the former Jewish quarter, writing many realistic essays about it, called *"Policing Prague's Pictures"*, describing the conditions there.

Neruda's life and work was greatly influenced by Malá Strana, he observed with wonder its beauty, atmosphere and inhabitants, and with a critical distance its conservatism. In Kampa, the park below Charles Bridge and one of the most beautiful places in Prague, Neruda met his great love, Anna Holinová, who lived at the house U Tří Zelených Křížů (Three Green Crosses), No. 16 U Lužického semináře. The house was the meeting-place of the literary figures of the day such as K.J. Erben and B. Němcová.

Particularly associated with Neruda's life and works is Nerudova Street where he spent his childhood and experienced his first loves, and he carefully recollected all the inhabitants and houses, even the names, in his *"Malostranské Stories"*. From the age four he lived at U Dvou Sluncù (House of the Two Suns), No. 47 Nerudova, where his father operated a tobacco shop on the ground floor. He went to school in Pohořelec.

On Nerudova Street, Czech patriots once met at the Kajetánské Theatre, and, in a nearby home in 1787, **Mozart** and **Casanova** once attended a ball.

In 1869 Neruda left Malá Strana, where he had spent 35 years of his life, and moved to the Old Town (Staré Město) to No. 28 Konviktská Street. Before he died, he lived briefly at No. 14 Vladislavova. He is buried in **Vyšehrad** Cemetery.

---

## ■ NEWSPAPERS AND MAGAZINES ■

Since 1989 there has been free development of journalism in the tradition of the 19th century similar to the period between the world wars when the daily press was influenced by personalities such as **Karel Čapek** and the presence of many cultural magazines and journals.

During **Communism** the press was unified and censored and many journalists could not participate. In the last half of the 1980's, the traditional periodical for the cultural public, the Lidové noviny, originally established in 1893, was distributed via "samizdat", a method of covertly hand copying forbidden texts. Of all the papers sold today the Lidové noviny is the oldest, the most popular are Mladá Fronta Dnes, Český Deník, Hospodářské noviny, and Telegraf. Tabloids, such as Blesk, are also popular in Prague.

Newspapers and periodicals for intellectual circles include Respekt, the colourful weekly Květy, Reflex, Mladý Svět, and art weeklies such as Literární noviny and bi-weeklies Ateliér, Divadelní noviny, Architekt, and more expensive reviews and periodicals. Economic developments may be found in the Ekonom, and Profit.

In the German language there is the weekly Prager Zeitung, Prager Wochenblatt, and Volkszeitung. English newspapers include the weekly Prague Post and The Central European Business Weekly, the bi-weekly Prognosis, and the monthly cultural arts forum X-Ink, etc. Detailed cultural programmes may be found in PRO (with German and English versions), and the Kulturní Přehled.

# ■ NEW WORLD (NOVÝ SVĚT) ■

The "New World" was a suburb outside the town wall
built by <u>Charles IV</u> around the Hradčany district, hence its
name. Many of its buildings were constructed during the
reign of <u>Rudolph the Second</u>.

<u>Tycho de Brah</u>e resided in New World before his
death at No. 76 in the house named "At the Golden
Griffin". The family of Giovanni Santini lived at the house
"At the Golden Acorn", No. 79, and fiddler František
Ondříček lived in the house "At the Golden Plowshare", at
No. 90. Artists such as Jan Švankmajer, a famous director
of animated <u>surrealist</u> films, and his wife, a painter, cur-
rently live in New World. There are many houses that ha-
ve the adjective "Golden" attached to their names such as:
"At the Golden Pear", No. 77, housing a well known re-
staurant; "At the Golden Grape", No. 78, possessing
a beautiful <u>Baroque</u> oriel; No.82, "At the Golden Tree";
No. 83, "At the Golden Bush"; No. 84, "At the Golden
Stork"; No. 85, "At the Golden Lamb"; No. 87, "At the
Golden Star"; No. 91, "At the Golden Crayfish"; and No. 92,
"At the Golden Sun".

The upper part of New World is adjacent to the Capu-
cin Monastery (its core is the Loreta). The Loreta was
a famous place of pilgrimage, being an architectural repli-
ca of the Loretan Chapel, which resembles the house of
the Virgin Mary of Nazareth. The monastery frontal was
built from 1721 to 1723, according to plans by K.I.
Dienzenhofer. In the centre is a tower with famous Ma-
ryan chimes from 1694. The central cathedral of the Birth
of the Lord is also Dienzenhofer's work. Loreta is popular
in part because its treasures are displayed publicly, including the Monstrance designed and created in Vienna in
1698 by architect Fischer of Erlach decorated with 8000
diamonds.

## ■ OBECNÍ DŮM (MUNICIPAL HOUSE) ■

At the beginning of the twentieth century the lack of suiable spaces for cultural activities was addressed by Prague's leaders in the decision to build a centrally located multi–functional municipal building at (today's) No. 5 náměstí Republiky, formerly the <u>Gothic</u> town palace of Czech kings. In 1903 proposals were solicited for its construction. The winner was the Czech Technical University Professor Antonín Balšánek (1865–1921), who was paired with the city's favoured architect Osvald Polívka (1859–1931). Luckily, the partnership was facilitated by similar artistic viewpoints: both were virtuous eclectics influenced by Vienna and Paris. The project was officially called "The Representative House of the Municipality of Prague", built between 1905 and 1912, according to the two architects' plans.

The Municipal House is a complex comprising of concert, exhibition and lecture halls, salons, restaurants, <u>cafes</u>, taverns, clubs and arcades. The prevailing style of the interiors is Viennese <u>Art Nouveau</u>, whereas the exterior is neo–Baroque, influenced by representative Parisian architecture of the second half of the 19th century (Le Petit Palais). Perhaps the most impressive parts of the building are its main entrance designed with a large metal marquee and the impressive cupola on the roof reminding the visitor that they are entering a cathedral of art.

The architects commissioned some of the finest artists of the age, such as the painters <u>Alfons Mucha</u>, Mikoláš Aleš, Max Švabinský, Jan Preisler, and sculptors Ladislav Šaloun, Bohumil Kafka and Rodin's pupil Josef Mařatka, to decorate the building.

# ■ OPEN AIR ■

The summer months of July and August are ideal for open air in Prague. Sporting is possible at the municipal swimming-pools (especially in Podolí at Prague's largest swimming-pool located at the south end of town). A cultural programme is traditionally organized and performed on Střelecký Island, consisting of theatre-fairs and "Theatre Island" (theatre performances, films, concerts, and garden restaurants).

Concerts are also organized in the unique gardens of the <u>Wallenstein Palace</u> in Malá Strana, using Sala terrena. Across the way from the Wallenstein Palace another Sala terrena, the Ledeburk Palace, is nearly remodelled where theatre performers and actors once played. Occasional concerts and cultural productions are held in the open air in the Old Town Square (Staroměské náměstí), in <u>Wenceslas Square</u> (Václavské náměstí), or at the <u>Prague Castle</u> gardens. The presence of many beautiful gardens and unique architectural gems invite a host of open air events to take place in the future.

# ■ OPERA MOZART ■

In central Europe, few young opera ensembles have reached the top as quickly as Opera Mozart. The original Prague Mozart company, according to the ambitious group's manifesto performs only interpretations of the genius' operas. By performing in locations historically linked to Mozart's life and in other creative ways, the company seeks to remind Prague's music lovers' of the close relationship <u>Mozart</u> had with the city, whose residents loved his *"Wedding of Figaro"* and, demonstrated moreover by his works specificly tailored to Prague's audiences, such operas as "<u>Don Giovanni</u>" (1787) and *"La clemenza di Tito"*.

The Opera Mozart continues the work of generations of outstanding Czech performers and also effectively ties together the spirit of Mozart's times with our own.

The first performances of Opera Mozart, in conjunction

with the experimental opera workshop Opera Furore, affiliated with Chamber Opera Prague, became the hit of the
1990's season. The performance, called *The Best of Mozart*, consisted of a medley of his most outstanding arias
staged by several innovative directors. Their overwhelm-
ing success was due to their excellent choice of lively and
temperamental future opera stars, the fine orchestra, and
outstanding stage directors such as Šimon Caban, Daniel
Dvořák, Petr Lébl, Jiří Nekvasil, Nina Vangeli and Daniel
Wiesner.

Other successful pieces followed such as *Figaro? Figaro!, Play Magic Flute* (an opera cabaret, a one–man show
of the Czech theatre star Vladimír Marek), Serail Live (director: Šimon Caban), and so on.

The Opera Mozart performs its chamber pieces at No. 1
Novotného lávka, in the **Smetana** Museum building near
the Charles Bridge, and, in the summer months, performs
at the historic **Stavovské divadlo** (**Estates Theatre**). The
pieces include Die *Zauberflöte, Cosi fan tutte, La Clemenza di Tito*, directed by opera conductor Jiří Nekvasil
in collaboration with set designer Daniel Dvořák.

Opera Furore, an experimental group of the Chamber
Opera Prague, has had similar success. An occasional laboratory for contemporary domestic opera performances,
Opera Furore was established on the eve of the **Communist** regime's demise in 1988 as an enthusiastic amateur
venture. The "opera that doesn't brake" was introduced
for the first time on February 2, 1989, at Malostranská beseda performing *Faust*, a work of the avant–garde composer Josef Berg. *Faust* was followed by: the post–industrial
opera T*he Violin Against Iron*, based on Purcell's *Abandoned Dido*; the very successful performance, The Most
Cursory Opera *Andy Warhol*, performed over 100 times;
a new piece by Hanuš Bartoň called **Golem**, performed
at the **Palace of Culture**. Opera Mozart and Opera Furore
are regularly included in the repertoire of Prague's theatre **festival**, the Mozart Open.

## ■ PALACE OF CULTURE ■

During "normalization", the period after the 1968 invasion of Czechoslovakia, many monumental buildings were constructed in Prague in accordance with the politically correct attitude toward socialism, the largest being the Palace of Culture at Pankrác Square near the **Baroque** citadel, **Vyšehrad**. Amidst limited competition in 1974 a mediocre design was chosen for political reasons from the Army Design Department which, together with the Hotel Forum, copied the urbanist idea of the Congressional Centre CCH in Hamburg (1969–73) which then resulted in the

*Palace of Culture (1976–81); Hotel Forum (1988) and Nusle Bridge (1973)*

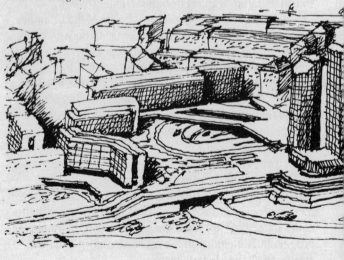

completion of the Palace of Culture in 1981.

It includes to large polyfunctional halls, smaller club rooms, cafes and restaurants. The interiors were designed by prominent Czech artists who changed it into a kind of gesamtkunstwerk of official 1970's Czech art. Certain foyers in the Palace of Culture offer outstanding views of some of the historical areas of Prague, particularly of its churches in the New Town, established in the fourteenth century by Kaiser **Charles IV** of Luxembourg.

## ■ JAN PALACH ■

Jan Palach, a student of the Philosophy Faculty of Charles University, immolated himself on January 16, 1969, on **Wenceslas Square** near the National Museum in protest against the Soviet Army's occupation of Czechoslovakia and the ensuing "normalization" by the **communist** government. He was taken to a burn center on Legerova Street where he died in three days later. His funeral on

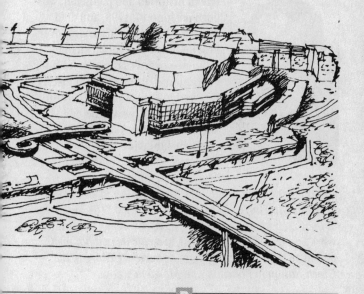

January 25, 1969, at Grave 89, Olšany Cemetery, served as a national protest against the occupying Warsaw Pact troops and against rigid communism. After his grave became a symbol of resistance, the Communists secretly exhumed his body and he was re–buried in Všetaty, his home town.

A month later on February 25, 1969, Jan Zajíc, an eighteen year old student at the railways technical school in Šumperk, also immolated himself on Wenceslas Square.

Although both suicide victims were discredited by the Communist government, twenty years later they became the symbol of freedom during the 1989 **Velvet revolution**. The square at the Philosophy Faculty was renamed Jan Palach Square in his honour and his death–mask, made of bronze by Olbram Zoubek, is placed on the building where he attended lectures.

## ■ FRANTIŠEK PALACKÝ ■

František Palacký, an outstanding Czech historian and politician, was born on June 14, 1798, and died May 26, 1876. After his arrival over Prague in 1823 he rapidly gained influence over Prague's scientific community. His interests in history resulted in the revision of certain museum practices and he edited various magazines such as the German–language *"Monatschrift der Gesellschaft des Vaterländischen Museums in Böhmen"* and the Czech–language *"Magazine Of the Society of the Patriotic Museum of Bohemia"*, later called *"The Magazine of the Czech Museum"*. In the 1830's, he began voluminous works on Czech history called *"Geschichte von Böhmen"* and in 1848 he began the famous series *"History of the Czech Nation in Bohemia and Moravia"*.

The momentum of his concept of Czech history was the struggle between the Slavic and Germanic elements, especially with respect to the Hussite period. According to Palacký it was during the Hussite period when the idea of the Czech nation prominently emerged. The main conceptual principles of State administration were formulated in Palacký's *"Idea of the Austrian State"* in 1865. Palacký's ideas are considered remarkable and topical, particularly his thoughts on a federation of central European nations. He urgently warned against the breakup of the Austria–Hungarian Empire because he considered a solid Danube state the best defense against powerful Russian and German neighbours.

Palacký's conception of a non–centralist Austrian state, however, met resistance with state authorities and he gave up his political office. In his later years he was rehabilitated and returned to his seat in the parliament.

His book *"A Brief History of Prague"* is very interesting for its popular description of Prague's development, significance and prospects. Palacký's life in Prague is associated with a petite palace at No. 719/7 Palackého Street at the corner of Jungmannova and Vodičkova, formerly the MacNewen Palace, which he gained through marriage and where he lived and died. The house was later inherited by his son–in–law, the famous politician František Ladislav Rieger, and is now maintained as a monument to Palacký and Rieger. Another impressive monument to Palacký was erected near Palacký Bridge, by Stanislav Sucharda, consisting of a complex of __Art Nouveau__ sculptures.

## ■ PASSAGES – MALLS ■

Around the 19th century it was common in the centre of Prague to design buildings with ground floor commercial space that had large open corridors in the interior connecting the store–front windows. The passages are mainly found particularly along __Wenceslas Square__, Vodičkova Street and Na Příkopě where the labyrinths provide easier pedestrian access to the centre. Some were included in designs by famous Czech architects, and although many are fragments of the original, they still retain their magic and beauty. One perceives in their appearance, the feeling of moving through the bowels of the centre, and many provide access to Prague's theatre's and cinemas.

Passages designed before World War I, such as the Ko-runa Pasáž on Wenceslas Square by architect A. Pfeiffer or Pasáž Lucerna off Vodičkova Street by architect **V. Havel**, are very interesting architectural conceptions.

In the spirit of the period between wars, purism and functionalism influenced designs along Wenceslas Square where there are designs by J. Gočár (No. 56) and L. Kysela (No. 28), on Na Příkopě (No. 31) by Antonín Černý, and on Štěpánská Street (No. 36) by E. Rosenberg. Some passages alternate narrow corridors with large interior squares, some with glass vaulted ceilings.

In some western countries it is a common architectural technique which has it's genesis in French and Italian galleries and the mall passages found in Prague.

---

## ■ ZDENĚK PEŠÁNEK ■

Zdeněk Pešánek (1896–1965) belongs to a group of Euro-pean kinetic art pioneers. An architect and sculptor, he is renowned as a creator of brave emotive complexes which unite noise, colour, light, and movement. His first work was shown in 1922 (Colourful Piano) and in 1926 he de-signed a war memorial for pilots by combining metal, glass, and the sound of aircraft engines. He exhibited the first kinetic object in Prague in 1930 which was placed on the Edison transformer building (Jindřišská Street).

A film called *"The Light Moves Through the Dark"* was made by Otakar Vávra, documenting this kinetic artwork. In 1937, he received a gold medal at the World Exposition in Paris for his fountain, which utilized light and kinetic effects. He re–collected his ideas about kinetic art in a book called *"Kinetism"*, printed in Prague in 1941.

# ■ PETŘÍN HILL ■

Petřín Hill (318 metres or 1043 feet high) is one the highest geographical points in Prague, located above Malá Strana, it overlooks many beautiful sights of Prague. The hill, originally the location of pagan sacrifices, was quarried in the early days for argillite, used as construction material for many of the **Romanesqu**e and **Gothic** buildings. The mining operations were rehabilitated with vineyards that in turn were replaced with **gardens**. There are well maintained pedestrian sightseeing paths, totalling two kilometres in length, originating at **Strahov Monastery**.

Petřín offers tourists many attractions: the Petřín Observation Tower (60 metres or 197 feet high), modelled from the Eiffel Tower and built for the Jubilee Exposition of 1891, held every 100 years at **Výstaviště (Exhibition ground)**; the nearby House of Mirrors, which resembles the Gothic **Vyšehrad** gate, was also constructed for the Expo, it contains a labyrinth of distorted mirrors and a dia–rama at its centre depicting the 1648 struggle between Praguers and Swedes on the Charles Bridge; and the Expo's funicular which starts at Újezd. The funicular, the longest in the Austria–Hungarian Empire when constructed, has a relief of 110 metres and has operated almost continuously since 1891. Today the upgraded funicular is capable of transporting 1,500 people per hour, with a single interim stop at the Nebozízek Restaurant located midway up the hill.

The Hunger Wall is by no means a negligible part of Petřín, the Gothic stone wall ranges up to 8 metres high and stretches over one kilometre from Strahov to Újezd. It was built between 1360 and 1362 in addition to Prague's fortifications, and part of it's legend states that **Charles IV** initiated the work to provide starving Praguers with jobs.

There is also an observatory on Petřín, opened in 1930, that currently houses a permanent astronomy exhibition.

The statue of the Romantic poet, K.H. Mácha, located

on the lower slopes of the orchard is a favorite meeting place for young romancing couples.

## ■ POSTIES AND YAP'S ■

The name Posties is a pseudonym which has been given to the generation of Americans who travel throughout the world to escape "the thought vacuum", a generation that may be considered "post–", as in post–sixties, post–sexual revolution, post–postmodernism, post–etc, many of whom have made their home in Prague. This phenomenon is described in numerous news articles and in a book by Douglas Coupland called *"Generation X"*. The mass media, in its lust for categorization and catchy acronyms, has promulgated the more specific term YAP's, meaning Young Americans in Prague.

The YAP's consist of mostly well educated young people who have a desire to write novels and poems, paint, compose, and practice various other arts. As journalist Chris Scheer noted, they have been coming to Prague from the first day **Havel** hoisted a **beer** at the **Prague Castl**e. In reality, the YAP's are not only Americans but foreigners from all over the world who reside in Prague and some estimate their numbers at 30,000. Some of the YAP's, such as Prague Post writer Alan Levy, believe that this period of time in Prague may be similar to living in Paris during the 1920's.

They are excited about the cultural, political and sexual attitudes, and appreciate the slow–paced and inexpensive lifestyle. They see Havel and Kundera as powerful symbols of the literary heritage of the Czech lands. Besides finding themselves through their art, they also teach and study foreign languages, practice trades from clothing design to journalism to photography, they have established writer and music groups, and do many other things they would not have the opportunity to do in places like New York City or Los Angeles.

This is a generation that accepts that they have less

financial opportunities than the previous generation and
who, instead of struggling in a dead-end job, have gone
on to places where they believe exciting things are happe-
ning. "We are looking for a movement, a change, life,
cultural history, a challenge. In this category Eastern
Europe is the biggest the world offers," says Scheer, the
founder of the English-language newspaper Prognosis.
To many foreigners the name of the Czech land itself, Bohemia, represents the land of the Bohemian lifestyle.

In addition to the more Bohemian-oriented YAP's, there are many political, law, economic, business, computer,
and educational experts, as well as entrepreneurs, resi-
ding in Prague, who are helping to slowly change the basic mentality and infrastructure of Prague for the better.
Since its beginnings, Prague has been a multinational city:
early documents speak of arab traders in Prague, Prague's
languages have included Latin and German as well as
Czech, Yiddish – there was formerly a Jewish quarter
called Josefov, Prague **Ghetto**, and French languages were common here, there are **Gothic** buildings designed by
the French and **Baroque** ones by the Italians (an Italian
quarter was formerly located at Vlašská Street in Malá
Strana), and Prague's culture has historically gained
strength through Jewish, German and Czech elements.

After World War II, however,the cosmopolitan aspect
of the city ended when the Jews were exterminated by the
**Nazis** and later when the Germans were expelled by the
**Communists**. The YAP's, therefore, represent one chance
at a new cosmopolitan Prague.

The YAP population is slowly but steadily integrating
into Czech society, as well as establishing their own
micro-community. There are three English language
**newspapers**: The Prognosis, The Prague Post and The
Central European Business Weekly, that provide current
news and information on Czech and foreign life in Prague.
There is a monthly cultural forum featuring Prague's
Czech and English-speaking art and essays, called X–Ink

Magazine, and other annual and quarterly journals such as Yazzyk and Trafika, and Gristlefloss, a compendium of random poetry and stories from presentations at "Beefstew", a poetry reading held every Sunday evening at the Radost Rock club.

There are several small English language publishing houses, notably the Twisted Spoon Press. Although foreign owned restaurants, **cafes** and **rock-clubs** come and go, some of the more popular include: McDonald's, Jo's Bar, FX Cafe (at Radost Nightclub), Red Hot and Blues, Cafe Nouveau, Martini Bar, Repre Club, Konvict Klub, Pizzeria Kmotra, Chicago's Pizza, Kamzík (boat restaurant), Andy's Cafe, Drake's (gay club), Cafe Kandinsky, The Globe, Derby's, Rock Club Borát, The James Joyce Pub, John Bull Pub, První Holešovická Kavárna and Hogo Fogo.

Some of the earliest pioneers on the post-revolution entrepreneurial scene in Prague, now defunct, included: Ubiquity, Cafe Delusion, New York Pizza, The American Centre cafe, The Thirsty Dog, The Irish Rover, and U Královské louky, Prague's first cafe-bookstore.

Cultural centres operated by various foreign embassies (for example U.S., British and French) offer excellent libraries and cultural events. Foreign language films, mostly English, are commonly shown at the U Hradeb cinema in Malá Strana, and English-speaking theatre troupes increasingly visit to perform on Prague's many stages. English-language videos may be rented at Video to Go. A number of weekly and monthly salons and mixers for people with specific interests are organized. There is also an English-language **radio** station, Radio Metropolis (106.2 Fm), and an American-style laundromat, Laundry Kings.

## ■ PRAGUE CASTLE ■

The Prague Castle was founded in 884-5 by Bořivoj, the first documented Czech prince. It was founded upon his return from Moravia where he had been baptised by

Methodius. He moved his encampments from Levý Hradec to the site of the future Prague Castle, where he built a sanctuary consecrated to the Virgin Mary which became the first church in Prague.

During the tenth century several other churches were built and the Prague Castle gained prestige as the ducal centre of the emerging Czech state. The earliest preserved written reports of Prague as a significant town were recorded by Ibrahim Ibn Jakub, an arabian Hebrew trader, diplomat, and travel writer. He visited the Czech lands in 965–66 and described Prague as a stone–built town with a viable international marketplace.

Since the 11th century, Prague Castle has undergone numerous changes to ensure the town's defense and to

*Vladislav Hall*
*of the Prague Castle*

promote its glory as a residential centre. A very important period of the Prague Castle was the reign of <u>Charles IV</u> and his son Václav, spanning from 1344 to 1419. Charles IV aspired to have his capital correspond to the status of his empire and the seat of Archbishop.

When the Hussite forces overran Prague in 1419–34, however, the Castle was devastated and fell to ruins until the reign of the Jagellon family at end of the 15th century who re-fortified it and built the superb Vladislav Hall and adjacent rooms.

When the <u>Habsburgs</u> came to the Czech throne in 1526 the Prague Castle was enriched with many styles of Italian <u>Renaissance</u> designs, particularly during <u>Rudolph II</u>'s reign, beginning in 1602. Once again it became a centre-piece of highest European culture and diplomacy.

In the mid 18th century, under Maria Theresa the Prague Castle acquired its present appearance, with the help of the Vienese architect N. Pacassi. Since 1918 the Castle

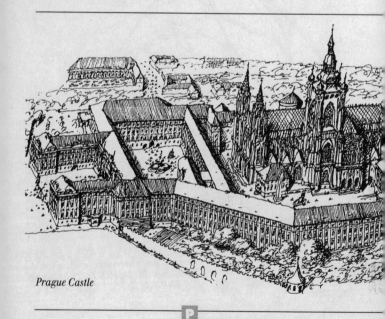

*Prague Castle*

has served as the residence and office of the nation's presidents. Today it is President **Havel**'s official residence.

## ■ PRAGUE LINGUISTIC CIRCLE ■

The lovers of literature, the experts and students of languages and language sciences are aware that Prague was the place where Czech structuralism was born. This aesthetic and historically artistic field of contemplation enjoys the interest of professional circles around the world. Although the theoretical and methodological roots of the movement resembled the Russian formalism movement, structuralism emphasized analysis of the work itself as well as dynamics and tension of the literary structure. (A set of theoretical essays on structuralist methods and some practical applications are published in the main work of Jan Mukařovský called *"Chapters form Czech Poetics"*).

The method of structuralism was conceived in Prague

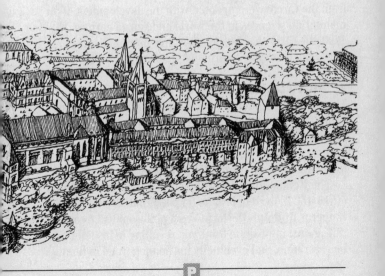

in the late 1920's, at the same time an association of linguists and literary theoreticians founded a group called the Prague Linguistic Circle. It was founded in 1926 by Vilém Mathesius, Jan Mukařovský, Roman Jakobson, Nikolaj Trubeckoj, Petr Bogatyrev, Bohumil Trnka, Josef Vachek, Bohumil Havránek, and René Wellek and others, for functional and structural research of linguistic and literary phenomena.

Theoretical foundations of the Circle can be seen in theses for the first slavistic congress in Prague (1929), in volumes of the series *"Travaux du Cercle linguistique de Prague"* and in the magazine called "Word and Belles lettres". This loose grouping developed eventually into the Prague School.

The liaison between the Russian formalist school and the Prague Linguistic Centre was Roman Jacobson, who worked in Czechoslovakia between the wars. They also associated with the pre–World War II avant–garde such as **Karel Teige**.

After 1948 their activities were halted, and Jacobson and Wellek emigrated to the USA. Structuralism and ideas from the Circle were updated with the development of humanitarian sciences in the world and since February 15, 1990, the Circle has been active once more in Prague under the honorary chairmanship of Professor Vachek.

## ■ PRAGUE'S PHILOSOPHERS ■

The names of numerous world famous philosophers are commonly associated with Prague, such as **Jan Hus**, **Comenius**, **T.G Masaryk**, **Einstein**, (all discussed in sections herein) and others. It is less commonly known that the following thinkers were intimate with Prague.

The **Renaissance** philosopher, Italian Giordano Bruno (1548–1600), lived in Prague for six months at the court of Emperor **Rudolph II**. His modern philosophical treatises ran against inquisition thinking, resulting in his long incarceration, and eventually his being burned in Rome.

Probably one of the most famous philosophers to be associated with Prague is Rene Descartes (1596–1650), who fought in Maxmilian Bavorský's army at the Battle of White Mountain, in 1620. He was wounded in the battle, which took place at the westerly end of Prague.

The logician, mathematician, and religious thinker Bernard Bolzano was born in Prague in 1781 and lived there all his life. His most important work *"Wissenschaftslehre"* was a defense against Kant on the possibility of objective knowledge, which was later expanded on by Franz Brentano and Edmund Husserl. Bolzano died in 1848 at No. 590/27 Celetná Street, at the house called "At the Four Stone Columns".

Another great mind of the twentieth century associated with Prague was Edmund Husserl (1859–1938), born in Prostějov (Moravia).

*Edmund Husserl*

## ■ PRAGUE SPRING ■

Prague Spring is not just a traditional music **festival**; but designates an attempt at political reforms in the mid–1960's by the **Communist** government of Alexander Dubček, whose slogan was "Socialism with a Human Face". Its aims were to achieve a more humanist, democratic, and politically–open socialist regime. This political process reached its apex in 1968, when leaders from the former Soviet Union, East Germany, Poland, Hungary, and Bulgaria perceived it as a counter–revolutionary threat. On August 21, 1968, the country was invaded by 600,000 soldiers from the Warsaw Pact forces.

After a period where the whole nation passively resisted the invasion, there began a long period of so–called normalization under President Gustav Husák, when approximately 500,000 people including Dubček were expelled from the Communist Party. Hundreds of thousands of others who agreed with Dubček, including many intellectuals, were dismissed from the jobs they were qualified for and were assigned to menial work. As a result, most Czech intellectuals, writers and artists were silenced.

---

## ■ PUPPET THEATRE ■

Puppet theatre began visibly in the 17th century during the **Baroque** era when puppet performances were developed by those in travelling shows. One of the legendary travelling puppeteers was Matěj Kopecký whose family carried on this tradition for generations. The marionette–style puppets were very popular during the early days and was the preferred entertainment of many villagers, and a strong puppet woodcarving tradition sprung up to supply this demand. Hand carved puppets are highly sought after today and there is a Museum of Puppets in Chrudim (approximately 100 kilometers east of Prague).

The original puppet repertoire was typically a light-hearted look at the classic theatre pieces such as Shakespeare, Marlowe, Gozzi, and Molière, the most popular being plays with international topics like *Faust, Jenovefa,* and *Don Juan.* By the beginning of the twentieth century, famous composers and artists were looking at the puppet theatre, for example, **Smetana** wrote preludes for the puppet theatre, M. Aleš, L. Šaloun, and V. Sucharda designed puppet sets and stages.

In 1929 the international puppet union, called UNIMA, was established in Prague with a huge exhibition and a theatre, called Empire of Puppets, opened in Prague especially for puppetry. The Empire of Puppets Theatre is located in the Municipal library building, in beautiful **Art Deco** style, and currently has lively performances from the National Marionette Theatre. A commerative plaque mounted on the building celebrates the founding of UNIMA. The National Theatre of Marionettes boasts one of the most popular and successful theatre performances in Prague since the 1989 **Velvet Revolution**, their **Don Giovanni**, under the direction of Karel Brožek in the classic marionette style of **Mozart**'s time, has been played a remarkable 700 times since 1991. The theatre also plays *Orfeo ed Euridice* by Ch. W. Gluck, a magical performance of Baroque stage technology.

*Ch.W. Gluck's Orfeo ed Euridice –Magic Theatre of Baroque World (National Marionette Theatre)*

Two other puppet theatres can be found in Prague. One is the professional Theatre of Spejbl and Hurvínek and the Theatre Minor. Prague's Academy of Performing Arts offers courses in the Department of the Alternative or Open Forms and Puppet Theatre with famous instructors such as professor Josef Krofta.

# ■ RADIO AND TELEVISION ■

Between the Great Wars, Czechoslovakia was among the ten most developed nations in the world and continuous radio broadcasting began here on May 18, 1923. After the Second World War and the **Communist** putsch in 1948, however, the nation backslid in the area of media technology. Tests for television broadcasting began May 1, 1953, and regular broadcasts began February 25, 1954. Colour television was introduced in the 1970's.

After the **Velvet Revolution** of 1989 and the peaceful split of Czechoslovakia, the new Czech Republic became the first former Eastern Block country to pass radio and television broadcasting laws comparable to those of the West. Article 10 of European Convention's on Human Rights provides the basis of the Czech Republic's broadcasting law, which provides each citizen with the right of free speech and information.

These new freedoms have led to prosperous growth of radio and television broadcasting. The first to take advantage of the new law was the underground music radio station called "Radio Stalin", currently Radio 1; there are presently twenty radio stations in Prague, compared to three stations during Communism, which include: three state–run stations (Český Rozhlas, Vltava, and Radiojournal) and the remainder are private, such as Europa 2 (FM 88.2), the first major station established in Prague with French cooperation, which broadcasts continuous music, news, moderated shows and advertising; Radio Golem (FM 90.3) which broadcasts cultural and social programmes concerning Prague, classical music, religious

programmes, daily and continuously on weekends; Radio
Metropolis (FM 106.2), an English-speaking station which
broadcasts popular music and programmes in conjunction
with the Voice of America; and others include Radio Kiss,
Radio Country, Radio Bonton, Radio Vox, Radio Classic,
etc. Three of the new stations broadcast throughout the
Czech Republic: Frekvence 1, Radio Alpha, and Radio
Echo. Radio Free Europe moved recently from Munich to
Prague, the BBC may be received at FM 101.1 and RFI
at FM 91.3 on the dial.

There are currently four television stations in Prague.
They include two state-run stations (Česká Televize,
Channel 1, and ČT, Channel 2) and two private stations
(TV Nova, Channel 3, covering the entire country, and TV
Premiéra, Channel 4, in Prague and central Bohemia).
There is also cable and satellite television, MTV, SKY,
RTL, SAT 1, PRO 7, and 3 SAT. The television signals are
broadcast primarily from the new television transmitter
in Žižkov (containing the view restaurant Emir-Hoffman),
from a tower located on **Petřín**, and a tower on Cukrák
hill south-east of Prague.

## ■ RENAISSANCE ■

Renaissance is an artistic style with its beginnings in Italy
around 1401 when in Florence a competition was established to create a bronze door for the baptismal Chapel
of St. John. The event represented a major detour from
paganistic artistic designs, which previously in the Middle
Ages had been assigned by decree, and all participants
were inspired by the antique. The name of the new movement, Renaissance, is found in the biographies of Italian
artists written by Michelangelo's student Giorgio Vasari.
In Italy the Renaissance lasted from the middle of the 15th
century to the mid-16th century when, after the final phase of the Renaissance called **Mannerism**, it was replaced
by the **Baroque**.

In the Czech lands the Renaissance appeared in the

*Star Hunting Lodge*
*(1556) – a rare work*
*of Prague's Renaissance*

late 15th century (the windows of Vladislav Hall in **Prague Castle**, 1493). It might seem strange but the Renaissance art of Prague was the work of foreign artists. The most famous work of Renaissance art in Bohemia is Belvedere, the King's countryseat in Prague, influenced by Venetian and Lombardian art. The chateau by the builders Paolo della Stella and Giovanni Spatio is generally considered the purist Renaissance architecture outside of Italy. The work was commissioned by the Czech King, Ferdinand I, for use by his wife and originally it was built with a dancing hall and richly decorated ground floor salons. Under **Rudolph II** the arcades of the house served as observatories for his astronomers. From there **Johannes Kepler** and **Tycho de Brahe** opened the skies for mankind to study the cosmos. In front of the Belvedere there is a unique "singing fountain", expertly cast by the Prague bellmaker Tomáš Jaroš according to a model designed by the graphic designer Francesco Terzio. Other

Italian art can be found in the nearby indoor Games Courts whose exterior is decorated with beautiful Sgraffiti.

Another odd work of Prague's Renaissance is the Hvězda chateau (Star Hunting Lodge) built on the west side of town in Liboc. It was designed and built by Archduke Ferdinand of Tyrolia, the son of King Ferdinand I. The chateau's floorplan is a six-pointed star, thus its name (Hvězda=star). The interior includes 334 stucco panels depicting events of Grecian mythology, considered the best of their kind outside of Italy. The Hvězda chateau attracted the attention of a group of **Surrealists**, led by André Breton through Prague in 1935.

Other superb Renaissance artworks in Prague include: the impressive Schwarzenberg Palace at No. 22 Hradčanské náměstí (the current Military History Museum); near the Hradčany townhall, the Martinický Palace at No. 67/8 Hradčanské náměstí; the marvellous "U minuty" house next to the Staroměstská townhall, again with superb Sgraffiti; the newly renovated Novoměstská townhall at Karlovo náměstí; and a unique complex of water towers near Jiráskův Bridge and **Mánes** Gallery building, the Staroměstská water tower at Novotného lávka near Charles Bridge, and the Lower Novoměstská water tower near Švermův Bridge.

## ■ RAINER MARIA RILKE ■

Rainer Maria Rilke, perhaps the greatest poet of the twentieth century, was born in Prague's New Town (Nové Město) on December 4, 1875. His family house at No. 17 Jindřišská Street was torn down and replaced with another structure in the 1920's (prior to that Rilke's mother lived in a house formerly located at the site of the department store mall called At the Black Rose).

Rilkes' family enjoyed going to a garden restaurant on Slovans Island (Žofín). They also strolled along Na Příkopě Street and on Saturday's along Švédská Street in Prague 5 – Smíchov, to the Rilke's uncle's villa Excelsior where they spent their summers. The poet often recalled his youthful days in Smíchov, his trips to Košíře, and peaceful walks through Malostranský Cemetery on Plzeňská Street. He attended piaristic gymnasium with **Franz Werfel** and **E.E. Kisch**. The poet sometimes read his poetry at the **Cafe** Arco.

Rilke, however, left Prague as soon as he was able to because he felt the intellectual sphere suffered from a stuffy greenhouse effect, he was oppressed by Prague's provincialism and by feelings of isolation in what he considered a language ghetto. He then drifted through Europe, living in France (where he worked as Rodin's secretary for a time in Paris), Germany, Italy, and Switzerland, where he is buried in a mountain cemetery.

Rilke's childhood experiences influenced his poetry and Prague itself is sometimes mentioned, places such as the **Prague Castle**, Loreta, and certain churches.

## ■ RIPELLINO AND PRAGA MAGICA ■

Prague is full of magical names and places and it is no wonder that so many people from around the world return again and again to explore the city, always finding something new and wondrous. The Italian Angelo Maria Ripellino is a case in point.

Ripellino (1923–78) was a Professor of Slavic Literature from Rome who visited Prague after Stalin's time, and he supported the few liberal Czechs in their hardships under **Communism** and he translated and promoted Czech literature in the West. In 1968 after **Prague Spring** he denounced the Warsaw Pact invasion in his essay *"Rats of the Regime"* and broke off his visits during the Soviet occupation. In 1973, he published Praga Magica, loaded with his knowledge and insight of Prague's culture, history and literature, and even the Czechs were fascinated by his clear-sighted story of their country. He depicted Prague as a viable metropolis and saluted its mystery, and his presence and concern represented for some Czechs a continuation of the Italian tradition following on from the <u>Re-naissance</u>, <u>Mannerism</u> and <u>Baroque</u> periods.

## ■ ROCK CAFES AND CLUBS ■

In addition to traditional <u>cafes</u>, first established in the 19th century, which play an important role in Prague's social and cultural life, another phenomenon, the rock–cafe or rock–club, has appeared on the Prague scene since the 1989 <u>Velvet revolution</u>. As a gathering place for Prague's youth, they serve as cafes during the day and have music venues in the evenings. The music programmes generally include local and foreign rock bands with varying reputations and quality, played in relatively small halls.

These new clubs and cafes often encounter public and private resistance, and have difficulties with licenses, rents, etc. The well known rock club Bunkr has struggled from the beginning against accusations of excessive noise, alleged drug use, etc. Some of these progressive cafes, have closed due to excessive pressure by inflexible city officials and property owners. Opening this style of modern cafe represents a real pioneering effort on behalf of the youth orientated (see: <u>Posties and Yap's</u>).

Large concerts are also becoming popular in Prague, held in large stadiums and arenas such as Strahov, Sport's Hall in Holešovice, Eden Hall, Sparta Stadium, and others. (A detailed listing of Rock cafes and Clubs is provided in the appendix.)

## ■ ROCOCO ■

Rococo prevailed in Czech architecture and decorations between 1740 and 1780, and it is commonly associated with the period of Maria Theresa. Its name is derived from the French term rocaille, a decorative motif which uses assymetrical stylized wings linked with a cock's comb.

The Rococo movement was based in Louis' France between 1710 and 1774. It is found primarily in interior decoration, particularly in rich ornamentations of gold, as seen for example in certain interiors of **Prague Castle**, in chateaus built in the mid 18th century outside of Prague such as Dobříš, Veltrusy, Hořín at Mělník, and in a number of Prague's palaces.

Norbert Grund (1717–67) is generally considered to be the most important Rococo painter to have worked in Prague; his work reflects European Rococo enriched with observations of natural daily atmosphere. Still–life paintings became popular at this time, and representative works of Kašpar Jan Hierschely and his teacher Jan Vojtěch Angermeyer are exhibited at the **National Gallery** in Jiřský klášter (St. George Monastery) at Prague Castle (Dept. of Czech Arts of the 18th Century).

The Rococo style strongly influenced Ignác Platzer (1717–87). Originally apprenticed in stone cutting under his father in Plzeň and later by Donner in Vienna, in 1743 he settled in Prague and founded a workshop which was continued by his offspring until 1913. Platzer sculpted the decorations of the Theresian wing of the Prague Castle, all interior plastic works of the St. Nicholas Church of Malá Strana, and a number of Prague's palaces such as the Sylva–Taroucca Palace at No. 10 Na Příkopě, Kaunic Palace at No. 15 Mostecká Street, and Kinský Palace at No. 12 Staroměské náměstí (Old Town Square). The small Sylva–Taroucca Palace is perhaps the most beautiful Rococo architecture in Prague.

# ■ ROMANESQUE ART ■

Romanesque art in Czech regions dates from the beginning of the 11th century to the mid–13th century. It is the last phase of the early Middle Ages. The name of the art is derived from the French l'art Roman to emphasize linkage between this style and other styles from Rome, and its connection to Latin languages. A typical Romanesque work is the Church of St. George at **Prague Castle**, with it's three–tier design also utilized in the design of the Church of St. Václav, in Prague 9 – Prosek.

The Czech Romanesque style is characterized by circular designs called rotundas originating from the Great Moravian tradition, a singular domestic architectural type. Three rotundas are preserved in Prague: St. Cross at Karolíny Světlé Street, St. Longin at Nové Město near the Church of St. Stephen, and St. Martin at **Vyšehrad**.

The Czech Romanesque art is preserved too in excellent handpainted books such as the masterpiece *"Codex of Vyšehrad"*, created in 1085 for the coronation of the first Czech King Vratislav. Prague contains some of the best preserved examples of Romanesque houses, particularly of their lower levels and vaulted ceilings. The outstanding

*Romanesque Church of St George and its Baroque front*

preservation of certain portions of residences constructed adjacent to the Vltava River resulted because as the river increased the height of its floodplain and flood–control weirs were installed requiring higher road elevations, the lower levels were subsequently converted to cellars and the first floors were converted to the entrance levels. Many of the buried cellars then were not subjected to later renovations. Romanesque architecture preserved in this way even includes former palaces such as The House of the Masters of Kunštát at No. 222 Řetězová Street, now publicly accessible, and the Romanesque former ground floor at No. 156 Husova Street, remodelled as a gallery.

Around Staroměstské náměstí at Celetná, Jilská, and Husova streets, there are approximately sixty Romanesque residences of this nature. The houses reaffirm a picture of Prague as a prosperous town of the late 12th century, already containing up to forty churches, six monasteries, and a stone bridge which was, according to a Prague chronicle of the day, built in three years beginning in 1158. The bridge's remains suggest it contained twenty one arches and was four metres lower than the Charles Bridge, built with sixteen arches in the same general area in the 14th century.

Other significant Romanesque sights in Prague include: the Black Tower with adjacent fortifications at Prague Castle; the crypt of the Břevnov monastery; portions of the Church of Virgin Mary Under–the–Chain (No. 1 Velkopřevorské náměstí, Prague 1); Church of St. Peter at Biskupská Street, Nové Město; the beautiful Church of St. Mary Magdalene at the edge of the town (Přední Kopanina, Prague 6); Church of St. John Baptist (Dolní Chabry, Prague 8); Church of St. Bartholomew, Kyje, Prague 9; and the numerous rotundas and little churches outside of town; all which affirm the immense value of the preserved Romanesque, the most ancient architectural style in the Czech lands.

# ■ RUDOLPH II ■

The Czech and Hungarian King and German Kaiser was born in 1552 in Vienna and died in 1612 in Prague. The eldest son of Maxmillian II, he was raised as a Catholic in the Spanish Court. In 1572 he was coronated with the Hungarian Crown, and in 1575 he was presented with the Czech Crown and elected Roman King. After the death of his father in 1576 he assumed rule.

Rudolph II was not married and so he had to oppose family wishes to have his brother Matthew elected in his place. In 1599 he developed a mental disease and his brothers established an interim government headed by Matthew. In 1601 Rudolph II recovered and then relapsed again in 1605.

Through the Libeň Peace Rudolph II maintained governmental control only in Bohemia and Silesia. The Czech states forced him to issue an Imperial charter in 1609 which guaranteed religious freedom for the Brethren Unity. In 1611 he was forced to resign.

Rudolph II was interested in the sciences such as mechanics, scientific devices, mathematics, astronomy, the arts including painting, gilding, plastic arts, jewelrymaking, mysticism, astrology and alchemy, crafts such as watchmaking, metalmaking, glassmaking, and nature. He employed dozens of artists, artisans, and scientists, among who included **Tycho de Brahe**, **Jan Kepler** and Thaddeus Hájek of Hájků. His financier was **Rabbi Löw**, who Rudolph II visited in the Jewish **ghetto**. His Court painters included Bartholomew Spranger, Hans von Aachen, **Arcimboldo** and sculptor Adriæn de Vries. The number of alchemists working for Rudolph II has been estimated at two hundred, including Jeronym Scotus and John Dee.

The world famous collections of Rudolph II included works of the Italian Masters Leonardo da Vinci, Michelangelo, Rafael, Caravaggio, Titian, and Cranach Sr. and Albrecht Dürer. His collections also included weapons, minerals, jewels, archeological pieces, rarities, animal morphology, various mechanical toys and machines; for example a perpetual motion mobile and precious astronomical instruments.

The collections decayed over time and as the last blow, at the end of the Thirty Years War when General Königsmark occupied the Castle and Malá Strana, all that remained was removed to Sweden.

*Prague Castle in the age of Rudolph II (1606)*

## ■ JAROSLAV SEIFERT ■

A great poet, Seifert is the only Czech to win the Nobel Prize for Literature (1984). He was closely related to Prague.

Seifert (1901–86) entered the literary scene with proletarian poetry (*The Town in Tears*, 1921) and other books where he expresses admiration for modern technology and new opportunities, and he was active in the avant–garde between the great wars. He was a member of Devětsil, which means Nine Powers, and he led a new artistic movement following **Dadaism**, which developed in the Czech lands concurrently with **Surrealism** in France, called Poetism. This movement is reflected by his work: *On The Waves TSF*, *Nightingale Sings Poorly*, and *The Male Pigeon*. Supporters of the movement included **Karel Teige** (also a creator of new visually shocking typography, used for *On The Waves TSF*), and the poet V. Nezval.

During the Second World War, Seifert's poetry and journalism was inclined toward a resistance to fascism and war. He discovered large national figures such as **Jan Neruda**, Božena Němcová, and his own patriotism in his collection *Turn the Lights Off*.

In the 1960's he wrote melodious, virtuous verses and at the end of his life, in his collections of free verse, he seeks answers to human existence and stresses the importance of love and home in one's life.

During the period of greatest **Communist** oppression Seifert continued his outstanding civic and artistic contributions and he represented an unyielding integrity for the Czechs, despite knowledge that during the 1950's his earlier avant–garde colleagues had been brought up before political tribunals, jailed or had simply disappeared. He continued to show his moral fibre during the Russian occupation in 1968 and during the normalization period of the 1970's, when he was among the founders of Charter 77.

The early creative years of Seifert's life are associated with Žižkov, an industrial quarter of Prague, he also lived near the Dalibor Tower of the **Prague Castle** and later in the villa suburb Břevnov. His memoir *All the Beauties* of the World makes delightful reading.

## ■ SEMAFOR THEATRE ■

Semafor is a theatre group of the 1960's which is still active. Its activities began in 1959 in Ve Smečkách, presently the **Činoherní Klub**, and from 1962 to 1993 the troupe performed in Alpha Palace (a Functionalist–style building, ca 1928, on **Wenceslas Square**, where **Surrealist** theatre performances were first presented by Jindřich Honzl in 1934. After the Communist putsch of 1948, the theatre, called New Theatre, was occupied by Prague actor, singer, director Oldřich Nový, a musical comedy star between the wars.).

Semafor remained on Wenceslas Square for three decades, its popularity being highest during its first ten years when Semafor (SEdm MAlých FORem or Seven Small Forms) specialized in musical comedy, jazz, film, poetry, pantomime, puppetry, and artwork, and presented many theatrical and musical greats, including the author/actor duo Jiří Suchý and Jiří Šlitr. After the death of Šlitr in 1969, Jiří Suchý remained popular during the Russian occupation and so–called normalization because the audience knew Suchý was persecuted and banned in the media or from publishing.

Jiří Suchý still leads Semafor, and because the theatre has been undergoing remodelling since 1993 the group plays in various theatres in Prague such as Ka Theatre.

Suchý is a revered poet and a lyricist of a thousand songs,
dozens of hits, and also playwright, author, scriptwriter,
actor and singer, theatre manager and talent agent for
Prague's theatre and show biz.

## ■ BEDŘICH SMETANA ■

Many of the great musicians whose
destinies and careers are linked to
the music–loving city of Prague have been affected by the personality
of **Mozart**, and before his name and
art became synonymous with the
Czech struggle for independence
and self–expression, Smetana often
sat behind the piano at salons and
concert halls and played Mozart's
music. In one of his critical essays
on Mozart, Smetana, an educated musicologist, organizer
of musical events, and publicist, said that Mozart was an
immortal master, that his **Don Giovanni** was a "musical
monument", and that Mozart's pearl of opera is *the
Wedding of Figaro*.

In the musical creations of Smetana, Prague is symbo-
lic of the independent Czech nation. High on a rock above
the Vltava the panoramic view from the **Prague Castle** re-
veals the silhouette of the legendary **Vyšehrad**, the hero
of the first symphonic poem *"My Fatherland"*, dedicated
to the King's town of Prague.

He also composed the cute comical opera *"The Bartered Bride"* a world famous opera still very popular in the
Czech lands.

Temperamental and nationalistic, Smetana was
a member of the Public Guards in the 1848 Revolution and
he composed several fighting marches. The revolution in
the streets of mid–19th century Prague provided the impetus for his first opera *"Brandenburgers in Bohemia"*. His
later opera *"Dalibor"* spoke of a young striker who was

incarcerated in Prague Castle. The opera *"Libuše"* was set in the earliest times of the legendary Vyšehrad and the princess Libuše who lived there became a symbol of the Czech nation.

At Novotného Lávka near Charles Bridge, there is the Bedřich Smetana Museum, with his statue in front. Smetana lived at Lažanský Palace (presently the Film School FAMU) from 1863–9, where he had a music school and also composed *the Bartered Bride* and *Dalibor*, from where he observed the construction of the **National Theatre** where they were played. He used to work as a choir director in the **secese** Hlahol building on the river front where there is a commemorative plaque.

---

# ■ STALIN'S MONUMENT ■

Perhaps one of the more bizarre works of Prague's **Communist** monuments of the 1950's, it encouraged by the cult of Joseph Stalin, it was manifested not only by the Hotel International and large tomb–like housing estates (panelaks) but by a huge statue of the man himself trailed by underlings located at Letenské Sady overlooking the Vltava River on line with the projection of Pařížská and Svatopluk Čech Bridge.

This statue, the world's largest, was unveiled in 1955 after the dictator's death. Seven thousand cubic meters of granite was quarried in northern Bohemia to form 31,753 blocks, weighing 14,021 tons, for construction of the complex of figures. Six hundred workers built the foundations, statues and surroundings. The complex of statues were completed by twenty three stonemasons. The stone Stalin measured 15.3 meters high, some 13.7 meters taller than Stalin in the flesh, while the whole structure measured some 30 meters in height. The entire complex covered 10 hectares of park land. The foundation included a series of catacombs built below the level of Letenská Plain which were used as storage rooms and shelters for the Ministry of the Interior, the Government, the Castle administration, and the Soviet Embassy. The Praguers nicknamed the monument "the meat market queue".

In 1961, under Khrushchev's campaign to discredit Stalinism, Moscow ordered the monument to be destroyed and it was blown up in 1962.

The sculptor Otakar Švec (who with his partners Jiří and Vlasta Štursa won the competition against sixty other teams and individuals) committed suicide just prior to the unveiling and even today his death is an enigma. His death may have resulted from personal problems or may have been associated with anonymous letters he received during the era's political trials, accusing him of servicing a murderer or possibly a secret police assassination of Švec who may have witnessed too much. What is known is that the sculptor's death was not unveiled until well after the statue was.

Later, the underground rooms, once depicted by a stone mason as a matter for Egyptian pharoahs, were used

*Stalin's Monument (1955)*
*– the world's largest*

for potato storage. After November 1989, some illicit underground artistic actions occurred there and Radio Stalin (currently **Radio** One) began broadcasting from there. Today homeless people are living beneath the abandoned pedestal, and they have a beautiful view of Prague, especially the Old Town.

## ■ STATE OPERA ■

The State Opera House is one of the three opera houses in Prague. The State opera House is built on the spot former-ly occupied by the wooden New Town Theatre which was built in 1859 and torn down in 1885 because it was a fire hazard. The Czechs had recently built **the National Theatre** and the Germans felt a new theatre was needed because their **Stavovské Theatre** was too small. The Neues Deutsches Theater was built in 1885-7 by the fa-mous Viennese construction firm Fellner und Helmer per the design of Viennese architect Karl Hasanauer who also designed the Burg Theater in Vienna.

In their efforts to have the grandest theatre in Prague, the Germans succeeded with the State Opera House. It opened January 5, 1888, directed by Angelo Neumann, with **Wagner**'s opera Meister Singers of Nuremburg, and performances included opera cycles of Mahler, **Mozart**, and Gluck, and classic dramas of Shakespeare, Goethe, Ibsen, and Schiller. Caruso sang at the theatre twice in 1904, the Petersburg Ballet and Tairov Theatre per-formed, in 1906 Strauss's Salome, in 1908 Debussy's Pelleas et Melisande was played, Max Reinhardt's famous Oedipus in 1911, Jedermann in 1912 and and the religious mystery Das Mirakel from 1913 with actors A. Moissi and P. Wegener. After Neumann, the theatre directors inclu-ded Alexander Zemlinský (1911-27), a student of Gustav Mahler who taught Arnold Schönberg (Zemlinský's broth-er-in-law). Zemlinský presented the world première of expressionism play Father by Hasenclever in 1915, and The Drums at Night by Brecht in 1923. After 1933, the theatre was an enclave of exiled German artists, the last democratic German theatre was closed when the **Nazis** marched into Prague.

After the Second World War, in 1945–6, the theatre was called Opera of the Fifth of May Theatre and, in 1946–8, the Big Opera Fifth of May. The theatre was placed under the **National Theatre** during **Communist** rule and operas of the National Theatre were played here. The opera conductor Václav Kašlík and stage designer Josef Svoboda were renowned during this period.

In 1992, the State Opera House became independent from the National Theatre and focused and still does primarily on opera and plays Verdi, Puccini, Offenbach, **Beethoven**, and Wagner in their original languages.

Unfortunately, exceptionally poor urban planning has resulted in this beautiful gem being virtually buried between the main highway, a parking structure and the boxy parliament building.

## ■ STEAMBOATS ■

Steamboating began in Prague in 1817 when inventor Josef Božek put a 13 metre beam mounted with a steam engine and paddlewheel in the Vltava River at Kaiser's Mill (Stromovka). Due to a lack of resources development of the steamboat did not proceed until May 1, 1841, when the first steamer, the Bohemia, was launched in the Vltava. The first tests of the steamer between Rohan Island and Libeň were sucessful but steam passengers were still required to go by horse and carriage to Obříství to catch a steamer on the Elbe to go to Dresden.

In 1857 the City of Prague purchased a German steamer, named Mescery, which on its maiden voyage ran aground in Chuchle and sank two weeks later at Vrané. On November 6, 1864, the Prague steamboating company was established, which began operation one year later, in August, when the first boat Praha–Prag left from Podskalí on its maiden voyage. Prague's mayor, V. Lanna, and

František Dittrich were the impetus behind the flotilla. In 1891, a steamer was named after Dittrich, and this famous steamer plied the waters for sixty years.

After the 1989 **Velvet revolution**, Prague's steamboating company has re-appeared (PRAGUE PASSENGER SHIPPING Ltd. – The oldest steamship company on the river Vltava), steamers cruise the Vltava between spring and autumn, and can be boarded at the main dock under Palacký Bridge (Rašínovo nábřeží, Prague 2) for regular transportation service and topical trips.

## ■ STRAHOV MONASTERY ■

The Strahov Monastery was established by King Vladislav II in 1140 and gets its name from its location– it guards the entry to the **Prague Castle**. It is anchored by the Abbott's Church Nanebevzetí Panny Marie, completed in 1182, a three-nave basilica with a single crossing nave. After several remodels the Church obtained its present day **Baroque** appearance, the work of Anselmo Lurago, in 1743–52.

On the easterly and southerly side of the Church the **Romanesque** character of the original monastery may still be discerned beneath the Baroque remodelling. The monastery is unusual for it extent and height, which makes it one of the more significant representatives of Romanesque times. The Premonstratensians initiated many cultural and scientific activities, as can be seen in its two large libraries in the collections of theological and philosophical literature. The most attractive part of the monastery is the Philosophy Hall decorated with beautiful ceiling frescoes of the *"History of Mankind"*, painted by the important Austrian Rococoist A. F. Maulbertsch in 1794. It also has an interesting gallery that contains one of the most famous German **Renaissance** paintings, the *"Rosary Celebration"* by Albrecht Dürer, purchased from the Church by the **National Gallery** in 1934, and one of the Gallery's most prized possessions.

At the monastery's entrance at Pohořelec, King

*Front of the Strahov
Monastery*

**Rudolph II** built the Chapel of St. Roch between 1602–12,
interesting for its post–Gothic style.

The monastery with its library of more than 130,000
antique books was restituted back to the Premonstratensians after 1989.

# ■ STUDIO YPSILON ■

Studio Ypsilon belongs to Prague's class of small eccentric
theatres. The small theatre troupe was first established in
Liberec during 1963–78 under Jan Schmid, a stage designer, author, actor and theatre director who put together the outstanding talents and unusual texts (*Encyclo-
pedias entry Twentieth Century*; H. Rousseau: *The Visit of
the Exhibition 1889*; Picasso: *Desire Caught by the Tail*),
collected improvisations, exaggerated opera (*Carmen Not
Only by Bizet*; Verdi: *La Traviata*; and Verdi: *Rigoletto*,
etc.) and encyclopedic catchword plays (such as *Michelangelo Buonarroti*; *Life and Death of K.H. Mácha*; **Jaroslav
Hašek**).

The actors group consists of comic personalities with
musical ability who after three decades have developed the
unique style of Jan Schmid (who is without a doubt one of
the most eccentric on the Czech theatre scene). Today Studio Ypsilon is located at No. 16 Spálená Street, Prague 1,
and includes many successful performances on its repertoire that often travel to foreign countries as well (for
example, **Mozart** *in Prague*; Woody Allen: *God*; Franz Kafka: *America*; I.A. Diamond: *Some Like It Hot*, and others).

# ■ JOSEF SUDEK ■

Josef Sudek (1896–1976) was a trained bookbinder who
became a photographer after the First World War when
he lost his hand. He studied at the State Graphics School
from 1922 to 1924 under Karel Novák, and after gradua-
tion he participated in the Czech Photographic Society.
Between 1926 and 1936 he worked with the Družstevní
Práce Publishing House as a photographer of adverti-
sements, portraits and landscapes, and published his photos in the periodicals Panorama and We Live.

His handicap led to his use of straight negatives measu-
ring 40 by 30 cm and Sudek used a Kodak Panoramic ca-
mera dating from 1894 to photograph his book called *Prague Panoramic* (1959).

SURREALISM /161/

The work of Sudek fills over twenty books, the most famous include: *St. Vitus* (1928), **Prague Castle** (1947), *National Museum Lapidarium* (1958), and *Janáček's Hukvaldy* (1971). Josef Sudek is among the world's most renowned photographers and is recognized as such in many exhibitions and art auctions. The originality of his work is especially light and his subjects become unreal illusions or have magical drama using long exposures.

He belongs to the social group of Prague's eccentrics, enjoying its exhibitions and concerts. Sudek lived in an old wooden studio in the garden at No. 24 Újezd at the base of **Petřín Hill**, and he had a nice old record collection that he enjoyed playing for his friends every Tuesday for many years.

## ■ SURREALISM ■

After **Cubism** and **Dadaism**, modern twentieth century art turned to Surrealism. Surrealism concerns the juxtaposition of incongruous fantastic elements and imagery to create art that provokes the imagination. It was first named by Apollinaire in relation to his play *Breasts of Tiresius* (1916) and the concept was further developed in the 1920's by French artists such as A. Breton, P. Soupault, P. Eluard, L. Aragon, B. Peret, and R. Crevel, who brought it alive with their art, films, theatres and theoretical manifestos.

From France Surrealism moved to international circles and to the Czech lands where it was embraced by Nezval and **K. Teige**. Close contacts between Prague and Parisian artists firmly established Surrealism in the Czech lands. The unique Odeon publishing house, established in 1925, worked with many avant-garde artists and published numerous surrealistic works. In 1926, surealistic theatre was played in the Liberated Theatre under the director of J. Honzl, J. Frejka, and **E.F. Burian** who also put on surrealist performances (including *Hamlet the Third*) in his own theatre D34. In 1932, a large *Poetry '32* exhibition

S

*Paul Eluard, Vítězslav Nezval and André Breton in Prague (1935)*

was held in **Mánes** gallery with the likes of Arp, Dali, Ernst, de Chirico, Janoušek, Klee, Masson, Miró, Muzika, Štyrský, Tanguy, Toyen, and Wachsmann.

In 1934 a surrealistic group of Czech artists formed and printed *The Manifesto of Surrealism* of Czechoslovakia (authored by Nezval, and Teige, the poet Biebl, the painters Toyen and Štyrský, the sculptor Makovský, the composer Ježek, and the theatre director Honzl were the founding members) and published other items such as *Surrealism Under Discussion, International Bulletin of Surrealism*, Andre Breton: *What's Surrealism?, Surrealism Against The Stream*, and the almanac *Neither Swan Nor Moon*, such magazines as *Zodiac, Revue Surrealism*, and *Epoch*, and organised speeches by Breton and Eluard. The surrealistic New Theatre was established in 1935 in the Alfa Palace (later **Semafor** theatre) that performed Breton and Aragon's *The Treasury of Jesuits*, and Nezval's *The Oracle of Delphi*. Both performances were directed by

J.Honzl, stage design by J. Štyrský, and music by J. Ježek.

The surrealist group disbanded in 1938 before the Second World War, but Teige had a small group of interested young intellectuals and artists who continued the surrealistic ideas even through times of **Nazi** and **Communist** persecution, and we can still see their influence on art today in the texts of **Bohumil Hrabal** and movies of Jan Švankmajer who continues to promote surrealist art at his gallery Gambra at the **Prague Castle** (**New World**).

## ■ SYNAGOGUES ■

The former Jewish **ghetto,** located north and northwest of the Old Town Square, once contained nine synagogues, built at different times and having different styles. They were utilized for Jewish religious worship, meetings, and teaching. The renovation of the ghetto at the end of the nineteenth century reduced the number of synagogues to six, five being nearly original. The Old–New Synagogue is the only one currently used for religious purposes while the others serve as exhibition halls and depositories of the State Jewish Museum.

*Old–New Synagogue and the Ghetto*

The proper Jewish service reflects itself in the interior design of the synagogues. In the middle of the east wall of the chapel there is the box for the Torah, and the pulpit, later exchanged for the reading stand, which is situated in the middle. The women's galleries are interesting too because the women do not participate in the men's service.

The Old–New Synagogue is the oldest in Europe (the oldest synagogue in the world being in Jerusalem). It was built in 1275–80 in an Early <u>Gothic</u> style and has served continuously for 700 years. There are many legends sur-

*The Old–New Synagogue is the oldest in Europe (1275–80)*

rounding it, including its being brought by angels from Jerusalem.

Another important synagogue in Prague is the Pinkas Synagogue at No. 3 Široká Street which was a private house of prayer for wealthy families, rebuilt in **Renaissance**-style from its original Late Gothic style, and after the Second World War it became a memorial of the 77,297 Czech Jews killed during the **Nazi** occupation. The Klaus Synagogue, No. 1 U Starého Hřbitova, which is built adjacent to the Old Jewish Cemetery wall, where **Rabbi Löw** taught Talmud, contains the collections of the State Jewish Museum.

Maisel Synagogue was built in 1590–2 with the permission of **Rudolph II** as a private synagogue for Mordechai Maisel. When the ghetto was torn down, the synagogue was renovated in a New Gothic style and currently houses the Museum collection. In front of the Old–New Synagogue, the Jewish City Hall contains the High Synagogue, a Renaissance building whose construction was also funded by Mordechai Maisel and which is also a Museum space.

The sixth synagogue in the Josefov area of Prague is the Spanish Synagogue, No. 1 Vězeňská Street, originating from 1605, but was remodelled in Pseudomaur style in 1867–8.

Since the end of the eighteenth century during the liberalization of the laws regarding the Jewish population synagogues were built outside the ghetto as well, for example, the Jubilejní Synagogue, No. 7 Jerusalémská Street, an exotic **Secese**-maur style, which is currently in use.

The only modern synagogue is the Smíchovská Synagogue, at No. 32 Stroupežnického Street in Smíchov, renovated in Functionalist style in 1930 by the architect Leopold Ehrmann.

# ■ KAREL TEIGE AND THE AVANT-GARDE ■

Alongside <u>A. Mucha</u> and F. Kupka, Karel Teige (1900–51) is one of the most significant and world famous representatives of Czech modern art. It is interesting that while Teige was active as a painter and graphic artist he became famous for his architectural and creative arts theory as well as his support for modern literary trends (poetism) and typography.

In 1920, Teige cofounded Devětsil, a left–wing artists group. In 1922, he met Le Corbusier in Paris his future (1929) adversary in terms of function, beauty, and grandeur in modern architectural theory. Unlike Le Corbusier, Teige was an uncompromising functionalist who saw architectonic beauty as something decadently aesthetic, refusing grandeur as an instrument of mental oppression. In 1925 he visited the USSR, and, from 1930–1, he lectured at the Bauhaus in Dessau on his cycle called *"On the Sociology of Architecture"*, assessing architectural developments of the 19th and 20th century from a Marxist viewpoint. Teige's avant–garde bias was reflected in his building commissions, for example Teige's Neo–Renaissance family home at No. 14 Černá Street was remodelled in the Purist style by Jaromír Krejcar in 1928. In 1938 Teige commissioned a new house at No. 5 U Šalamounky per the Functionalist design of Jan Gillar.

Teige held the opinion that architecture should create a rational scientifically sound basis for the life of modern man lyrically crowned with modern poetry and paintings. In the later part of the twenties Teige co–created Czech

Artificialism, a modification of European Non–figurative painting based on unusual softening of abstract creative speech and associating capabilities. In 1934, with the famous Artificialist painters J. Štyrský (1899–42) and Toyen (1902–1980), Teige founded the Group of **Surrealists** in the Czechoslovak Republic. The group established contact with Andre Breton who visited "Magic Prague" in 1935, and in the same year the group, with Breton, issued the *Bulletin International du Surrealisme* and prepared several other interesting publications. Within this framework Teige created collages inspired by Max Ernst's work and initiated in the late thirties a vicious dispute with Stalinism from the standpoint of leftist Marxism. The last years of his life he spent in a close circle of young Prague surrealists unable to publish or defend himself against attacks by Czech toadies of Stalin. He died of a heart attack on October 1, 1951, and shortly thereafter two women friends committed suicide.

## ■ TROJA CHATEAU ■

The unique **Baroque** areal, the magical compositions of its gardens– the beautiful Troja Chateau was built as a summer residence for the Sternberg family. It was designed by the Frenchman Jean Baptist Mathey and built in 1679–85, styled after Italian country chateaus near Rome. The facade is united with the garden by a monumental staircase, lined with statues (created between 1685 and 1703 by the two Dresden sculptors George and Paul Heermann, with Italian influences), an art piece that unites Czech Baroque with Italian art centres. The interior decorations are conceptual of Flemish Rubensque paintings and the central hall is the work of Antwerp painter Abraham Godyn and his brother Isaac. The adjacent halls contain ceiling frescoes by the Italian artist Francesco Marchetti and his son Giovanni. The terraces with the large vases made of fired clay in front of the castle, were designed in the French garden styles of the 17th century.

There is a permanent exhibition of the Prague Municipal Art Gallery on display in the chateau. Its beautiful country–like setting and its proximity and view of **Prague Castle**, its position in the low hills above the Vltava and the surrounding vineyards, across from the Zoo, its huge park with fountains, labyrinth, orangery, and summer theatre, makes it a dominating architectonic feature.

Its complete renovation, begun in 1977, was undertaken with the idea of the Chateau as representative of the prominence of the **Communist** Czech nation. However, after the election of the purist J. Andropov as leader of the USSR, the Prague Communist Party toned down their extravagant plan.

*Troja Chateau – the unique Baroque areal (1679–85)*

# ■ UNGELT ■

Ungelt is an enclosed housing complex in the Old Town neighbourhood built at the former Princes' homestead as a secure centre for foreign traders since the <u>Romanesque</u> times. The name comes from duties (ungelt) which were also paid here. It was fortified in the tenth century and contained a hospital and the Church of St. Maria. It formerly occupied the area between today's Old Town Square and the Church of St. Jacob, and was also known as Týn, the name later taken for the Church of St. Maria on Staroměstské náměstí. Early historians consider this area to be the original centre of Prague– the Celtic word Týn being correlative with the English word town.

Ungelt, in certain old memoirs, was also known as laeta curia, a Latin word meaning "happy courtyard". For centuries the town's constables, not to mention its citizens, were only allowed in if unarmed. Today's Ungelt keeps its original courtyard character with two gates, one an entrance facing Týn Church, secured by cannon portals, and contains the Granovský House which is one of the most important urban <u>Renaissance</u> buildings in Prague, built in 1560 for tax collector Jacob Granovský of Granov. The house opens into the courtyard via an arched loggia with extraordinary paintings depicting Greek and Biblical events and, on its lower portion, a painting depicting bacchanalia and a portrait of King Ferdinand I. The neighbouring house forming the adjacent wing is also Renaissance, built for J. Strada, <u>Rudolph II</u>'s collections curator. After the ongoing renovations are completed Ungelt will once more serve as an important cultural centre.

# ■ THE VELVET REVOLUTION ■

There are two key political events affecting the life of **Communist** Czechoslovakia. The year 1968, the time of the **Prague Spring**, when the revival of a more humane socialist process was interrupted by the invading armies of the Warsaw Pact countries, led by the USSR which resulted in a neo–Stalinist interdiction lasting over twenty years. The other critical year was 1989 when on November 17th a peaceful, hence "velvet", revolution began which lead to the overthrow of the Communist government and to the gradual installation of a parliamentary democracy.

On November 17, 1989, about 15,000 students took to the streets to commemorate events that occurred on the same date in 1939, when the student Jan Opletal was shot dead by the **Nazis**. Participants of the 1989 student rally requested fundamental social changes, a dialogue with Party representatives, and called for the basic principles of democracy, liberty and human rights. At the intersection of Narodní Street near the department store Máj, currently K–Mart, there was a tough clash with police units, called up by the Communist Party, who used truncheons, dogs, water hoses and armoured personnel carriers against the students. The action resulted in 143 injured and over 100 arrests.

The next day rumours spread through Prague that one student had been killed. Spontaneous demonstrations then began in central Prague as most of Prague's theatres went on strike to establish solidarity with the students and force democratic changes.

On November 19th a large rally took place on **Wenceslas Square** without serious police intervention.

On November 20th the college students of Prague occupied the schools and were joined by students outside of Prague who began to occupy schools outside of the capital. About 150,000 people assembled in the city centre threatening to demonstrate with general strikes.

On November 21st the General Secretary of the Communist Party Miloš Jakeš pleaded with citizens to remain responsible and calm, at the same time the Communist Party prepared to actively suppress the revolution. A very large demonstration again took place on Wenceslas Square and the students, theatre employees, and intelli-

*Alexandr Dubček and Václav Havel on November, 1989*

gentsia were this time joined by factory workers and la-
bourers. For the first time **Václav Havel**, a highly persecuted critic of the regime, a playwright, a dissident, and
a founder of the opposition movement Charter 77, appeared before the public and spoke.

On November 25th the demonstrations were moved
from the city centre to Letná, a large parade ground, where a record 750,000 protestors gathered to support the de-
mands formulated by the future leaders of the Civic Forum. The 1968 General Secretary Alexander Dubček and
Havel were among the speakers.

The next day a similar demonstration took place at
Letná, with the Communist Party leadership no longer in
power.

On November 27th a general strike was held, the student strike continued, previously banned political parties
became active once again, and the government was forced
to negotiate. The Civic Forum was established for negotia-
tions as a wide people's front in favour of democracy. This
social force played a significant role in the revolutionary
days and months to come. The Forum's spokesmen called
for punishment of those responsible for the Národní Street
confrontation and for the removal of compromised officials from the political scene.

At the Federal Assembly meeting of November 29th the
Constitutional monopoly by the Communist Party was
abolished and an investigatory body of the Národní "mas-
sacre" was initiated.

On December 3, a new government was put forth that
included too many Communists for the public to accept.
Another government was established that was headed by
Prime Minister Marián Čalfa and the then–President Gus-
táv Husák resigned office. On December 11th the
three–week strike by actors ended but the student strike
continued. On December 20th Dubček was elected
Chairman of Parliament and with the election of Václav
Havel as President on December 29, 1989, the November

revolution was officially over. He was later inaugurated at Vladislav Hall in **Prague Castle**.

The Velvet Revolution was special for its remarkable calm and bloodless transition of governments particularly in light of the superpowers anxiously watching from the sidelines. Moreover, the form of the revolution was characterized by a theatrical or carnival–like atmosphere highlighted by several leading dissidents, personalities, notable students and actors.

## ■ VETERANS ■

The worldwide wave of interest in old technical items and industrial architecture is now catching up in Prague, a capital with many industrial and technical traditions. Between the wars it is worth remembering that Czechoslovakia was among the top ten developed countries and that in 1918 Bohemia and Moravia were the most industrialized areas of the Austro–Hungarian Empire. The connoisseurs of technology enjoy the large collections of the National Technical Museum at No. 42 Kostelní, Prague 7–Holešovice, which include surface (road and rail) and air transport, photography and cinematography, astronomy and time measurement devices, electronics, even mining equipment in a one kilometre long tunnel.

In addition to the Technical Museum, vintage automobiles are on display at the special AutoMuseum Praga, which focuses on autos produced by the Praga Automobile Company. The AutoMuseum includes several dozen richly documented autos manufactured between 1908 and 1965. Reservations (addressed to Mr. E.O Příhoda, No. 14 Vrátkovská, Prague 10, tel. 777644, or Mr. R. Příhoda, No. 658 Lamačova, Prague 5) are required to view the private Praga collection. A collection of autos from the Brno car manufacturer Z (Zbrojovka) can be seen by appointment by contacting the poet/owner Petr Cincibuch (tel./fax: 733470). Other vintage auto clubs include AutoClub of the Czech Republic at No. 29 Opletalova, Prague 1, and the

Veteran Car Club of the Czech Republic at the same
address; and Czechoslovak Club of Historic Vehicles
at PO Box 305, No. 14 Jindřišská, Prague 1.

A Museum of Prague Mass Transportation has been recently established near **the Prague Castle** using an
authentic tram garage to house the collection. In 1875 the
first trams were operated using horse power, the first
electric rails were used in 1891, and the first bus lines were established in 1908, connecting Malostranské via Nerudova Street to Pohořelec. Dozens of similar exhibits, mostly of trams, trolley buses and buses, are also on display in
the halls of Střešovice tram garage at the intersection of
Patočkova and Střešovice Streets. In addition, certain
historical vehicles (ie. trams) are sometimes put back into
action on the streets of Prague during special occasions.

The Museum of Aviation and Aerospace, located at the
Kbely Airfield, displays more than fifty old aircraft in its
halls and fields, contains exhibits of space research, and
also has tanks and other combat equipment mostly from
the second World War period. The military is also the topic of the Military History Museum at No. 2 Hradčanské
náměstí, Prague 1, and the Museum of the Czechoslovak
Army at No. 2 U památníku, Prague 3–Žižkov.

## ■ VIEWPOINTS ■

Prague is set in a hilly and dissected terrain that offers
many views and panoramas of the city. Perhaps the favorite and most beautiful viewpoint is from the beautiful
"Little Eiffel" tower at the top of **Petřín Hill** which over-

looks the oldest portions of Prague and its many church steeples. It is here, from Petřín's tower in clear weather, the Krkonoše Mountains at the northerly–most part of the Czech lands may be seen.

The Hradčanské Square of **Prague Castle** provides another very pleasant view over Malá Strana, and other pretty views include **Strahov Monastery**, Letenské Orchards, especially where the **Stalin Monument** once stood, and from **Vyšehrad**. Other good high view points includes: the hills of the Smíchov district, Kavčí Hory (home of Czech Television); and, in the centre of Prague, there are the Riegerovy Orchards, where historical Prague can be seen close up, and Vítkov Hill in the Žižkov district.

Other excellent places to view Prague, are from the historical towers, such as the Old Town City Hall Tower, the Powder Tower near **Obecní dům**, and the towers of Charles Bridge, and from certain high buildings, particularly the Forum and Panorama Hotels, and from the new television tower, containing a view restaurant, in Žižkov.

## ■ VYŠEHRAD ■

Since the early Middle Ages the city of Prague has been situated between two fortified hills. The fortified hill overlooking the bridge was named simply the Castle and the other, upstream of the Castle on a steep rocky cliff above the Vltava River, was called Vyšehrad. Although the story of Vyšehrad is rife with legends of how it was once the cradle of the ruling Přemysl family, however, according to certain archeologists, Vyšehrad actually post–dates the Castle.

Since the tenth century the Vyšehrad was controlled by Czech dukes, and its connecting road to the Old Town and Castle, the present–day Spálená and Vyšehrad Streets, was an important trade artery. In 1070 the Vyšehrad was converted from a wooden to stone fortification which contained churches including a house independent of the Prague Bishop and subordinate only to the Pope. Vyšehrad gained great importance during the reign of **Charles IV**, who deemed that coronations of the newly elected king should include a journey from Hraďčany to Vyšehrad to assure that both power centres were recognized.

During the Hussite wars the Vyšehrad was sacked and never regained its former glory. After Westphalian peace broke out in 1648, the Vyšehrad was thoroughly re–fortified and transformed into a miltary base that included underground corridors and casemates.

The Vyšehrad's attractive features today include: the **Romanesque** Rotunda of St. Martin, the Church of St. Peter and Paul, founded by Duke Vratislav II before 1129 and remodelled in a **Gothic** style under Charles IV and again by purist architect Mocker in 1885–7, and when the Vyšehrad was converted to a **Baroque** fortress in 1660, a cemetery was founded under the incentive of the patriotic priest provost, Václav Štulc, to accomodate the most significant Czechs, dominated by the monumental Mausoleum Slavín which serves as a common tomb for about six hundred outstanding Czechs such as **Smetana**, **Dvořák**, **Destinnová**, **Mucha**, Aleš, Mácha, **Neruda**, **K. Čapek**, and others. In addition to its pious mission, the Vyšehrad cemetery has become a gallery of famous sculpture represented by works of Myslbek, Štursa, B. Kafka, Šaloun, Španiel, Sucharda, **Bílek**, and so on.

*Vyšehrad before 1420*

## ■ RICHARD WAGNER ■

"The ancient magnificient beauty had a remarkable effect on my imagination and expression," the famous German composer Wagner noted after several stays in Prague, despite its being an arduous three-day journey from Dresden by stagecoach. He first visited when he was young, and fell in love in Prague. After 1834 he stayed several times at the Hotel "At the Black Horse" on Na Příkopě (formerly Staré Aleje and Kolovratská) where the famous Italian violinist virtuoso Niccolo Paganini stayed in 1828, as well as the Norwegian composer Edvard Grieg, in 1903 and 1905. The hotel site is currently occupied by the National Bank, and today the street is very busy, so much so that it is hard to believe it was once so quiet that these illustrious visitors once questioned passers-by as to the whereabouts of Prague's downtown business district.

Wagner was in Prague during the revolutionary year of 1848 to introduce his operas *"Tannhäuser"*, *"Lohengrin"*, and *"Der Fliegende Holländer"* and *"Rienzi"* at the <u>Stavovské Theatre</u>, and also conducted concerts of portions of his work at Žofín Island.

## ■ WALLENSTEIN PALACE ■

The Wallenstein Palace is generally considered to be the beginning of the <u>Baroque</u> in Prague. At the same time it represents Prague's second most important architectonic areal, after the <u>Prague Castle</u>, and combines a unique Baroque garden with the palace. Along with the <u>Troja Chateau</u> its construction is included among the works of Albrecht of Wallenstein (1624–30), a tragic figure of European history, especially of the Thirty Years War.

Inside the Palace one may imagine the setting of Schiller's famous drama, and the atmosphere surrounding the ambitious warrior Albrecht who cloaked himself in the greatest luxuries of the age. In order to establish a building site, the determined Albrecht had twenty six houses, three gardens and a lime kiln demolished, making way for his two Italian architects, led by Giovanni Pierroni, to build the palace. In the palace several rooms on the first floor are preserved, particularly the main hall called Knights Hall where concerts are currently held and where the final scenes of Amadeus, the film by **Miloš For-man**, were filmed. The hall is richly decorated with stucco containing depictions of certain geniuses and military insignia. The centre of the ceiling is painted with a portrait of Wallenstein mounted on a horse, as Mars the God of War, by the Italian painter Bacio Bianco.

A beautiful Baroque garden belonging to the palace is decorated with a sala terrena at the front, a monumental

*Wallenstein Palace and Garden*

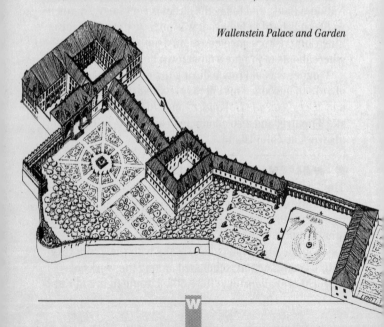

*Count Albrecht von Wallenstein*

loggia with Italian stucco designs and paintings, where **open air** concerts are presently performed. The opposite side of the garden is a former riding school, which now serves as an exhibition hall for **the National Gallery**. In addition to aviaries and grottoes, the garden also contains bronze statues of antique gods and horses designed by Adriaen de Vries to form a fountain, unfortunately finished after his death. In 1648, the originals were captured by the Swedes occupying Prague and now reside at the Drootningholm Royal Chateau near Stockholm. In front of the Loggia above the fountain there is a cast of the statue Venus With Amor, the original sculpted by the Nuremburg sculptor Benedict Wurzelbauer in 1599 and displayed at the Prague Castle gallery.

   In the former stables there is the Pedagogic Museum of J.A. Komenský (**Comenius**) and the palace itself is currently occupied by the offices of the Ministry of Culture.

# ■ CARL MARIA WEBER ■

Shortly after Mozart's time, **the Stavovské Theatre** hosted other world renowned musicians, in particular Hayden's student and pianist, Carl Maria Weber (1786–1826). He spent three years of his career in Prague during 1813 and 1816, as an opera conductor at the Stavovské. He produced a wide variety of opera, for example, he introduced *Fidelio* to Prague, and he continually raised the level of Prague's musical awareness.

Weber's opera *"The Magic Bowman"* with its Romanticist score and its storyline of the Šumava Forest continues to be very popular, and is commonly included in many Prague repertoires. At **the National Theatre** it has been produced 11 different times and each production played between 41 and 86 times. Weber was well known not only as an extremely gifted musician but also as a kind and friendly person.

# ■ ST. WENCESLAS ■

Wenceslas, the patron saint of Bohemia, was named a Czech prince in 921.

King Wenceslas was a devout Christian and his religious beliefs influenced much of his governing. His positive relationship with the Germans, however, led to a strong Czech resistance led by his brother Boleslav. In 929 at a church at his castle in Stará Boleslav, Boleslav and his assistants assassinated the good King Wenceslas. Wenceslas's body was taken to Prague and buried in St. Vitus Cathedral.

Wenceslas, as a martyr, achieved the status of sainthood and became the patron saint of Bohemia. He became a legend and many songs and fables grew up around him, and the St. Wenceslas song is still sang as a national prayer in certain churches; the King's jewelry is consecrated in his name and Prague's main square with its equestrian statue is dedicated to him. The space around St. Wenceslas's statue has been a rallying point for many important demonstrations and gatherings in the twentieth century.

### ■ WENCESLAS SQUARE ■

A Horse Market, a Cattle Market and a Hay Market, or the present–day Wenceslas, Charles and Senovážné Squares respectively, anchored the New Town being built by **Charles IV**. These Squares were the main centres of Prague at that time extending from **Vyšehrad** to the Old Town. The present name "Wenceslas Square" was first suggested in 1848 by Karel Havlíček Borovský "to honour our old kind patron **saint Wenceslas**". A so–called Prokopská Gate and later Horse Gate once stood at the location of the National Museum at the top of the Square, but was demolished in 1875. Originally the square was unpaved, and its upper part, after **Rudolph II**'s time, contained a gallows where agitators and moneylenders were publicly executed.

The lower part has been known from the thirteenth century as Na Můstku or On the Little Bridge because there was an entryway from the Old Town. When the Metro was constructed the original stone bridge was uncovered.

The dominant structure of Wenceslas Square is the National Museum (1885–90), designed by Joseph Schulz who also worked on **the National Theatre** and the Rudolphinum. The top consists of a cupola covering a ceremonial hall called the Pantheon, a national sanctuary containing sculptures of the most important figures of Czech culture.

Facing the square across from the Museum is a statue of St. Wenceslas designed by J.V. Myslbek symbolizing national strength. Myslbek worked on the statue from 1890 until his death in 1922.

One of the more important buildings of the square is Hotel Evropa, designed by Dryák and Bendelmayer in 1906, a beautiful example of Czech **Art Nouveau**. Constructed in the same spirit are the Hotel Ambassador at No. 5/840 on the lower part and same side as the Hotel

Evropa and the Koruna office building on the nearby corner with its tower resembling a crown.

The Art Nouveau architecture of Jan Kotěra, the so–called Peterka's House (No. 12/777), prepared the ground for the coming wave of modern twentieth century architecture.

There are two examples of Functionalist architecture in the neighbourhood, the Baťa building (No. 6/774) designed by L. Kysela and built in 1928–9, and the former Lindt building (4/773).

In the middle of Wenceslas Square there are two building complexes having interior "**passages**" or malls lined with storefronts, restaurants, bars and theatres, such as Palace Alpha (No. 28/785) designed in the spirit of modern Constructivism, and, on the corner of Štěpánská Street, The Lucerna building complex (No. 38/794), designed by the Havel family construction firm in 1912, and it has now been passed back to the family of **Václav Havel**.

In the central part of the Square at the intersection of Jindřišská Street, the former Assicurazioni Generali Insurance building is designed in an extravagant neo–Baroque style, interesting because **Franz Kafka** once crossed its threshold daily as an employee from 1907–08.

In the last days of the Second World War some buildings in the upper part of the Square were aerially bombed in "friendly fire" and were rebuilt, for example, the Supermarket at the intersection of Washington Street and House of Fashion at the intersection of Krakovská Street. The most valuable structure built in the 1950's is the Hotel Jalta designed by Antonin Tenzer.

Wenceslas Square, seen as the city's centre by Praguers, has become a place of joyous and sad events and rallies, from the Revolution of 1848 to the 1989 **Velvet Revolution**.

At the time of Le Corbusier's third visit in 1928 he remarked "that the Boulevard of Wenceslas Square is superb, its life and its tempo.."

# ■ FRANZ WERFEL ■

Franz Werfel (1890–1945), the poet and writer, was born in Prague and died in Beverly Hills, California. He was one of the most important German Expressionist poets. Werfel's more famous books include the novel *"Forty Days"*, *"Verdi"* a biography of the famous composer, *"Death of A Provincial"*, *"Secondary School Graduate's Reunion"*, and his plays *"Goats Singing"* and *"Jakobowski and the Colonel"*. Werfel became interested in Catholicism which is explored in his mystical novels *"The Song of Bernadette"* and *"Jeremiah"*.

Werfel attended a gymnasium on Štěpánská Street where he first met his long-life friend **Max Brod**. Later when he lived on Mariánská Street he had meetings there, inviting intellectuals and friends, including **Franz Kafka** and Brod. Werfel and Brod often took long walks through Prague, through its parks and woods, they made boat trips through the St. Johns stretch of the Vltava, and also travelled together to Karlovy Vary.

Many of the young German writers of his age, including **Rilke**, Kafka, Brod and Werfel himself enjoyed visiting and reading their work in progress at places such as the Montmartre **Cafe** (At the House of the Three Wild Men on Řetězová Street), Cafe Concordia, and The Continental on Na Příkopě.

Werfel was one of the public's more popular poets of the time; he married the widow of Gustav Mahler, but she left him after a short time for the architect Walter Gropius.

## ■ IMPORTANT PHONE NUMBERS ■

| | | |
|---|---|---|
| **Emergency calls Police** | | **158** |
| Traffic accidents | | 21 21 37 47, 42 41 41 |
| **Emergency Ambulance Service** | | **155** |
| Ambulance car | | 37 33 33 |
| First aid – 24 hours service / Prague 1, Palackého 5 | | 24 22 25 21, 24 22 25 20 |
| First aid for children – 24 hours / Prague 1, Palackého 5 | | 24 22 25 21, 24 22 25 20 |
| Emergency medical aid | | |
| | Department for foreigners | |
| | Prague 5 – Motol, | |
| | Nemocnice Na Homolce, Roentgenova ul. 2 | |
| | (24 hour service) | 52 60 40, 52 92 11 11 |
| Dental first aid | | |
| | Prague 1, Vladislavova 22 | 24 22 76 63 |
| | Prague 4, A. Staška 80 | |
| | (Underground C – Budějovická) | 692 89 43 |
| Pharmacy | (24 hours service) | |
| | Prague 1, Na příkopě 7 | 24 21 02 29, 24 21 02 30 |
| **Fire brigade** | | **150, 24 22 13 59** |
| Main Post Office | | |
| | Prague 1, Jindřišská 14 | 24 22 88 56 |
| Information for Prague numbers | | 120 |
| Information for numbers in the Czech Republic | | 121 |
| Alarm–clock by telephone | | 125 |
| Telegrammes by telephone | | 127, 0127 |
| Code numbers for abroad | | 0149 |
| Customs | | |
| | Prague 1, Havlíčkova 11 | 23 22 270, 24 21 28 85 |
| | Ruzyně Airport | 36 78 16, 334 31 00, 334 44 11 |
| Prague Information Service / Prague 1, Na příkopě 20 | | 54 44 44 |
| Yellow Angels – 24–hours emergency road service | | 154, 123, 0123 |
| Railways Information | | |
| | Wilson Railway Station | 24 21 76 54 |
| | Masaryk Railway Station | 24 22 42 00 |
| | Holešovice Station | 24 61 58 65 |
| Bus Information | | 22 14 45, 24 21 10 60 |

# ■ MUSEUMS ■

**THE NATIONAL MUSEUM – NÁRODNÍ MUSEUM**
Praha 1, Václavské nám. 68, tel.: 24 23 04 85

**NATIONAL LITERATURE MUSEUM**
Praha 1, Strahovské nádvoří 1, tel.: 2451 1137

**PRAGUE CITY MUSEUM – MUSEUM HLAVNIHO MĚSTA PRAHY**
Praha 1, Na Poříčí 52, ,tel.: 24 22 31 80

**CITY TRANSPORT MUSEUM – MUSEUM MĚSTSKÉ DOPRAVY**
Vozovna Střešovice – Praha 6, Patočkova 4
tel./fax: 32 23 349

**MUSEUM ART AND INDUSTRY – UMĚLECKOPRŮMYSLOVÉ MUSEUM**
Praha 1, ul. 17. listopadu 2, tel.: 24 81 12 41

**RUDOLFINUM – THE HOUSE OF ARTISTS – DŮM UMĚLCŮ**
Praha 1, Alšovo nábř. 12

**TROJA CASTLE – TROJSKÝ ZÁMEK**
Praha 7, Troja, tel.: 84 07 61

**THE STRAHOV LIBRARY – STRAHOVSKÁ KNIHOVNA/ STRAHOV MONASTERY**
Praha 1, Strahovské nádvoří 1/132
tel.: 24 51 03 55

**THE NATIONAL TECHNICAL MUSEUM – NÁRODNÍ TECHNICKÉ MUSEUM**
Praha 7, Kostelní 42, tel.: 37 36 51

**COMENIUS PEDAGOGICAL MUSEUM – PEDAGOGICKÉ MUSEUM JANA ÁMOSE KOMENSKÉHO**
Praha 1 – Malá Strana, Valdštejnské nám. 4
tel.: 51 32 453–7

## ■ THE MUSEUM OF CZECH MUSIC – MUSEUM ČESKÉ HUDBY ■

**ANTONÍN DVOŘÁK MUSEUM – MUSEUM ANTONÍNA DVOŘÁKA**
Praha 2, Ke Karlovu 20, tel.: 29 82 14

**MUSEUM OF BEDŘICH SMETANA – MUSEUM BEDŘICHA SMETANY**
Praha 1, Novotného lávka 1, tel.: 726 53 71

**JAROSLAV JEŽEK MUSEUM – MUSEUM JAROSLAVA JEŽKA**
Praha 1, Kaprova 10, tel.: 24 22 90 75

**BERTRAMKA – W. A. MOZART AND THE DUŠEK'S MUSEUM**
Praha 5, Mozartova 169, tel.: 54 38 93

## ■ STATE JEWISH MUSEUM IN PRAGUE – STÁTNÍ ŽIDOVSKÉ MUSEUM V PRAZE ■
Praha 1, Jáchymova 3, tel.: 24 81 00 99
**Permanent collections**
THE OLD JEWISH CEMETERY – STARÝ ŽIDOVSKÝ HŘBITOV
THE OLD–NEW SYNOGOGUE – STARONOVÁ SYNAGÓGA
THE PINKAS SYNAGOGUE – PINKASOVA SYNAGÓGA
(Memorial to the victims of Holocaust)
KLAUS SYNAGOGUE – KLAUSOVA SYNAGÓGA (Old Hebrew prints)
MAISEL'S SYNAGOGUE – MAISELOVA SYNAGÓGA (Silver of Czech Synagogues)
HIGH SYNAGOGUE – VYSOKÁ SYNAGÓGA (Synagogal Textiles)

## ■ THE MILITARY MUSEUMS ■

**THE MUSEUM OF MILITARY HISTORY – HISTORICKÉ VOJENSKÉ MUSEUM**
Praha 1, Hradčanské nám. 2, tel.: 53 64 88

**THE MUSEUM OF AVIATION AND SPACE TRAVEL – MUSEUM LETECTVÍ A KOSMONAUTIKY**
Praha 9, Kbely, tel.: 82 47 09

**THE MUSEUM OF CZECHOSLOVAK ARMED RESISTANCE – MUSEUM ODBOJE ČS. ARMÁDY**
Praha 3, U Památníku 2, tel.: 27 29 65

**THE POLICE MUSEUM – POLICEJNÍ MUSEUM**
Praha 2, Ke Karlovu 1, tel.: 29 89 40

**NÁPRSTEK MUSEUM OF ASIAN, AFRICAN AND AMERICAN CULTURES**
Praha 1, Betlémské náměstí 1

**THE POSTAGE STAMP MUSEUM – MUSEUM POŠTOVNÍCH ZNÁMEK – VÁVRŮV DŮM**
Praha 1, Nové mlýny 2, tel.: 23 12 660

**TOYS MUSEUM – IVAN STEIGER'S COLLECTION** / The Burgrave's Palace – Prague Castle (former House of Children)
Praha 1 – Hradčany, Jiřská 4

**THE LORETTO – LORETA** / The Loretto Treasure
Praha 1 – Hradčany, Loretánské náměstí 7
tel.: 53 62 28

# ■ GALLERIES ■

## ■ NATIONAL GALLERY IN PRAGUE – NÁRODNÍ GALERIE ■

**NATIONAL GALLERY IN PRAGUE – NÁRODNÍ GALERIE**
Praha 1, Hradčanské nám. 15, tel.: 35 24 41

**STERNBERG PALACE – ŠTERNBERSKÝ PALÁC**
Collection of old European Art, French Art of 19. and 20. Century
Praha 1, Hradčanské nám. 15, tel.: 2451 0594

**CONVENT OF ST GEORGE – KLÁŠTER SV. JIŘÍ** /Old Czech Art
Praha 1, Jiřské nám. 33, tel.: 24 51 06 95

**CONVENT OF ST. AGNES OF BOHEMIA – KLÁŠTER SV. ANEŽKY ČESKÉ**
Czech and middle European Art of 19. century
Praha 1, U milosrdných 17, tel.: 24 81 06 28

**PRAGUE CASTLE RIDING SCHOOL – JÍZDÁRNA PRAŽSKÉHO HRADU**
Praha 1, U Prašného mostu 55, tel.: 3337 ext. 3232

**KINSKY PALACE – PALÁC KINSKÝCH**
Graphic Collection
Praha 1, Staroměstské nám. 12, tel.: 24 81 07 58

**WALLENSTEIN RIDING SCHOOL
– VALDŠTEJNSKÁ JÍZDÁRNA**
Praha 1, Valdštejnská 3, tel.: 53 68 14

**ZBRASLAV CASTLE – ZÁMEK ZBRASLAV**
Sculpture Collection
Praha 5, Zbraslav, tel.: 59 11 88

**■ PRAGUE MUNICIPAL ART GALLERY
– GALERIE HL. M. PRAHY ■**

**OLD TOWN HALL
– STAROMĚSTSKÁ RADNICE**
Praha 1, Staroměstské nám. 1

**THE HOUSE AT THE STONE BELL
– DŮM U KAMENNÉHO ZVONU**
Praha 1, Staroměstské nám. 13, tel.: 231 02 72

**CITY LIBRARY – MĚSTSKÁ KNIHOVNA**
Praha 1, Mariánské nám. 1

**BÍLEK'S VILLA – BÍLKOVA VILA**
Praha 6, Mickiewiczova 1, tel.: 34 14 39

**TROJA CHATEAU – TROJSKÝ ZÁMEK**
Praha 7, U trojského zámku 1, tel.: 84 77 47

**■ CZECH MUSEUM OF GRAPHIC
AND PLASTIC ARTS ■**

**CZECH MUSEUM OF GRAPHIC AND
PLASTIC ARTS – ČESKÉ MUZEUM
VÝTVARNÝCH UMĚNÍ**
Praha 1 – Staré Město, Husova 19–21
tel.: 24 22 20 68–70

**CAROLINUM**
Praha 1, Ovocný trh 3, tel.: 22 88 441

**■ CZECH FOUND FOR THE PLASTIC
ARTS – ČESKÝ FOND VÝTVARNÝCH
UMĚNÍ ■**

**ČAPEK BROS. GALLERY – GALERIE BRATŘÍ
ČAPKŮ**
Praha 2, Jugoslávská 20, tel.: 25 89 96

**MÁNES GALLERY – GALERIE MÁNES**
Praha 1, Masarykovo nábř. 250, tel.: 29 55 77

**NEW HALL GALLERY – NOVÁ SÍŇ**
Praha 1, Voršilská 3, tel.: 29 20 46

**V. ŠPÁLA GALLERY
– GALERIE VÁCLAVA ŠPÁLY**
Praha 1, Národní 30, tel.: 22 47 09

**■ Dílo – Galleries ■**

**CENTRUM**
Praha 1, Národní 37, tel.: 23 26 134
**LETNÁ**
Praha 7, M. Horákové 22, tel.: 38 10 43
**NUSLE**
Praha 4, Nuselská 5, tel.: 43 41 53
**PLATÝZ**
Praha 1, Národní 37, tel.: 24 21 27 68
**U MOZARTA**
Praha 1, Uhelný trh 11, tel.: 24 21 28 29
**U SV. MARTINA**
Praha 1, Uhelný trh 11, tel.: 23 26 067
**ZLATÁ LILIE**
Praha 1, Malé nám. 12, tel.: 24 21 41 90

**ZLATÁ ULIČKA**
Pražský hrad, tel.: 53 67 65

**■ CENTRAL EUROPEAN GALLERY AND
PUBLISHERS – STŘEDOEVROPSKÁ
GALERIE A NAKLADATELSTVÍ ■**

**STŘEDOEVROPSKÁ GALERIE**
Praha 1, Husova 21, tel.: 24 22 20 68–70

**CENTRE OF CZECH GRAPHICS
– CENTRUM ČESKÉ GRAFIKY**
Praha 1, Husova 10, tel.: 23 27 940

**■ Other Galleries around Prague ■**

**IF – ART FASHION GALLERY**
Praha 1, Maiselova 21

**BEHÉMOT GALLERY**
Praha 1, E. Krásnohorské 1, tel.: 231 78 29

**ČESKÁ GALERIE – KLÁŠTER PREMONSTRÁTŮ
NA STRAHOVĚ**
Praha 1, Strahovské nádvoří 1/132

**DOBRA – FOTOGALERIE**
Praha 1, Kostečná 5

**ENTLER – DVOŘÁKOVÁ GALERIE**
Praha 1, Loretánská 8, tel.: 53 61 13

**GALERIE ARS BOHEMICA**
Praha 1, Řetězová 3
– Dům pánů z Kunštátu a Poděbrad

**GALERIE BÖHM**
Praha 2, Anglická 1, tel.: 23 62 016

**GALERIE FRONTA**
Praha 1, Spálená 53, tel.: 29 65 08

**GALERIE GEMA**
Praha 1, Husova 8

**GALERIE GENIA LOCI**
Praha 5, Újezd 11, tel./fax: 53 94 68

**GALERIE HOLLAR**
Praha 1, Smetanovo nábř. 6, tel.: 248 108 04

**GALERIE INFERNO**
Praha 1, Ovocný trh 12

**GALERIE JAROSLAVA FRÁGNERA**
Praha 1, Betlémské nám. 5A

**GALERIE JNJ**
Praha 1, Nerudova 26, tel./fax: 53 33 13

**GALERIE K**
Praha 2, Kateřinská 6, tel.: 29 37 17

**GALERIE K & B**
Praha 1, Jilská 7, tel.: 24 22 98 08

**GALERIE MIMO**
Praha 8, Sokolovská 67/1, tel.: 24 21 88 09

**GALERIE MLADÝCH „U ŘEČICKÝCH"**
Praha 1, Vodičkova 10, tel.: 24 21 36 18

**GALERIE MXM**
Praha 1, Nosticova 6, tel.: 53 15 64

**GALERIE NO.9**
Praha 5, Újezd 9, tel.: 53 72 08

**GALERIE PALLAS**
Praha 1, Náprstkova 10, tel.: 26 08 15

**GALERIE PASEKA**
Praha 2, Ibsenova 3, tel.: 25 53 27

**GALERIE PEITHNER – LICHTENFELS**
Praha 1, Michalská 12, tel./fax: 24 22 76 80

**GALERIE RADOST**
Praha 2, Bělehradská 120

**GALERIE ROB VAN DEN DOEL**
Praha 1, Jánský vršek 15

**GALERIE U PRAŽSKÉHO JEZULÁTKA**
Praha 1, Saská 3, tel.: 53 61 69

**GALERIE U PRSTENU**
Praha 1, Jilská 14

**GALERIE U TÝNA**
Praha 1, Staroměstské nám. 14/604, tel.: 231 49 36

**GALERIE VAVRYS**
Praha 1, Rytířská 11, tel.: 26 30 72

**GALERIE VIA ART**
Praha 2, Resslova 6, tel.: 29 25 70

**GALERIE VLTAVÍN**
Praha 1, Masarykovo nábř. 36
tel.: 24 91 45 40

**GALERIE 33 – BERGMAN**
Praha 2, Vinohradská 27, tel.: 62 72 179

**PRAGUE PHOTOGRAPHY HOUSE
– PRAŽSKÝ DŮM FOTOGRAFIE**
Praha 1, Husova 23

**STARONOVÁ GALERIE**
Praha 1, Maiselova 15, tel.: 23 21 049

## ■ THEATRES ■

**ARCHA**
Praha 1, Na poříčí 26, tel.: 23 21 370

**BRANICKÉ DIVADLO**
Praha 4, Branická 41, tel.: 43 05 07

**ČERNÉ DIVADLO JIŘÍHO SRNCE
– BLACK THEATRE
DIVADLO ZA BRANOU II
– OTOMAR KREJČA**
Praha 1, Národní tř. 40, tel.: 24 22 96 04

**ČINOHERNÍ KLUB – THE DRAMATIC CLUB**
Praha 1, Ve Smečkách 26, tel.: 24 21 68 12

**DEJVICKÉ DIVADLO**
Praha 6, Zelená 15a, tel.: 311 23 65 6

**DIVADLO FRANZE KAFKY – FRANZ KAFKA
THEATRE – DIVADLO V CELETNÉ**
Praha 1, Celetná 17, tel.: 24 81 27 62

**DIVADLO JIŘÍHO GROSSMANNA**
Praha 1, Václavské nám. 43, tel.: 26 46 88

**DIVADLO KOLOWRAT**
Praha 1 – Staré Město, Ovocný trh 6
tel.: 24 21 43 39, 24 22 85 03

**DIVADLO NA STARÉM MĚSTĚ**
Praha 1, Dlouhá 39, tel.: 23 14 534

**DIVADLO NA VINOHRADECH
– THE VINOHRADY THEATRE**
Praha 2, nám. Míru 7, tel.: 25 70 41

**DIVADLO NA ZÁBRADLÍ
– THEATRE ON THE BALUSTRADE**
Praha 1, Anenské nám. 5, tel.: 24 22 19 33

**DIVADLO POD PALMOVKOU**
Praha 8, Zenklova 34, tel.: 663 117 081

**DIVADLO SPEJBLA A HURVÍNKA**
Praha 2, Římská 45, tel.: 25 16 66

**DIVADLO V ŘEZNICKÉ**
Praha 1, Řeznická 17, tel.: 29 65 14

**DIVADLO ZA BRANOU II
– OTOMAR KREJČA
THE THEATRE BEHIND THE GATE**
Praha 1, Národní tř. 40, tel.: 24 22 96 04

**DUNCAN CENTRE**
Praha 4, Branická 41

**HUDEBNÍ DIVADLO V KARLÍNĚ
– MUSIC THEATRE IN KARLÍN**
Praha 8, Křižíkova 10, tel. 24 22 75 14

**LABYRINT**
Praha 5, Štefánikova 57, tel.: 54 50 27

**LATERNA MAGIKA
– NOVÁ SCÉNA– THE NEW STAGE**
Praha 1, Národní tř. 4, tel.: 24 91 41 29

**LYRA PRAGENSIS**
Praha 1 – Lobkovický palác
– Pražský hrad, Jiřská 3, tel.: 53 73 06

## MĚSTSKÁ DIVADLA PRAŽSKÁ
## – PRAGUE MUNICIPAL THEATRE

**DIVADLO ABC**
Praha 1, Vodičkova 28, tel.; 24 21 59 43

**ROKOKO – ČINOHERNÍ STUDIO**
Praha 1, Václavské nám. 38, tel.: 24 21 71 13

**DIVADLO „K"
– KOMORNÍ DIVADLO KOMEDIE**
Praha 1, Jungmannova 1, tel.: 24 22 24 84

**MINOR**
Praha 1, Senovážné nám. 28, tel.: 2421 3241

**MIRACOLOUS THEATRE OF THE BAROQUE
WORLD – ZÁZRAČNÉ DIVADLO
BAROKNÍHO SVĚTA**
Praha 1, Celetná 13, tel./fax: 232 41 89

**NÁRODNÍ DIVADLO
– THE NATIONAL THEATRE**
Praha 1, Národní tř. 2, tel.: 24 91 26 73

**NÁRODNÍ DIVADLO MARIONET
– NATIONAL MARIONNETTE THEATRE**
Praha 1 – Staré Město, Žatecká 1, tel./fax: 232 2536

**OPERA MOZART**
Praha 1, Novotného lávka 1, tel.: 245 11 026

**SEMAFOR**
Praha 1, Václavské nám. 28, tel.: 24 22 76 92

**STÁTNÍ OPERA – STATE OPERA**
Praha 2, Wilsonova 4, tel.: 24 22 76 93

**STAVOVSKÉ DIVADLO
– THEATRE OF ESTATES**
Praha 1 – Staré Město, Ovocný trh 1, tel.: 2421 4339

**STUDIO GAG – BORIS HYBNER**
Praha 1, Národní tř. 25, tel.: 24 22 90 95

**STUDIO YPSILON**
Praha 1, Spálená 16, tel.: 29 22 55

**VIOLA**
Praha 1, Národní tř. 7, tel.: 24 22 08 44

**ŽIŽKOVSKÉ DIVADLO T. G. MASARYKA –
DIVADLO JÁRY CIMRMANA**
Praha 3, Štítného 5, tel.: 62 78 900

## ■ CONCERTS ■

**CZECH PHILHARMONIC – RUDOLFINUM**
Praha 1, Alšovo nábř. 12, tel.: 24 89 33 52

**PRAGUE SYMPHONY ORCHESTRA–FOK**
Praha 1, nám. Republiky 5, tel.: 23 22 501

**ATRIUM**
Praha 3, Čajkovského 12, tel.: 62 70 453

**BERTRAMKA**
Praha 5, Mozartova 169, tel.: 54 38 93

**HLAHOL HALL**
Praha 1, Masarykovo nábř. 16

**JANÁČEK HALL**
Praha 1, Besední 3

**KŘIŽÍK FOUNTAIN – KŘIŽÍKOVA FONTÁNA**
Praha 7, Výstaviště – Exhibition Grounds

**KLEMENTINUM – THE CHAPEL OF MIRRORS**
Praha 1, Mariánské nám.

**LICHTENSTEIN PALACE**
Praha 1, Malostranské nám. 13/258

**LOBKOVIC PALACE**
Praha 1, Pražský hrad, Jiřská 3

**NOSTIC PALACE**
Praha 1, Maltézské nám. 471
tel.: 245 11 285, 24 51 04 52

**SMETANA HALL OF OBECNÍ DŮM**
Praha 1, nám. Republiky 5

**VINOHRADY NATIONAL HOUSE**
Praha 2, nám. Míru 9

**ST. AGNES CONVENT – ANEŽSKÝ KLÁŠTER –
KOSTEL SV. FRANTIŠKA**
Praha 1, U milosrdných 17

**BASILICA OF ST. JAMES**
Praha 1 – Staré Město, Štupartská ul.

## ■ LIBRARIES ■

**NATIONAL LIBRARY**
Praha 1, Klementinum 190, tel.: 26 72 41

**MUNICIPAL LIBRARY**
Praha 1, Mariánské náměstí 1, tel.: 28 31 111

**STRAHOV LIBRARY** / Strahov Monastery
Praha 1, Strahovské nádvoří 1, tel.: 2451 0355

## ■ CINEMAS ■

**AERO**
Praha 3, Biskupcova 31, tel.: 89 36 01

**ALFA**
Praha 1, Václavské nám. 28, tel.: 22 07 24

**BLANÍK**
Praha 1, Václavské nám. 56, tel.: 23 52 162

**HVĚZDA**
Praha 1, Václavské nám. 38, tel.: 26 45 45

**JALTA – DIF CENTRUM**
Praha 1, Václavské nám. 43, tel.: 24 22 88 14

**KVĚTEN**
Praha 2, Vinohradská 40, tel.: 25 33 41

**LUCERNA**
Praha 1, Vodičkova 36, tel.: 24 21 69 72

**PAŘÍŽ**
Praha 1, Václavské nám. 22, tel.: 24 22 01 59

**PASÁŽ**
Praha 1, Václavské nám. 5, tel.: 26 73 89

**PONREPO**
Praha 1, Národní tř. 40

**PRAHA**
Praha 1, Václavské nám. 17, tel.: 26 20 35

**PRAŽSKÝ FILMOVÝ KLUB**
Praha 1, Václavské nám. 17

**SEVASTOPOL**
Praha 1, Na příkopě 31, tel.: 26 43 28

**SVĚTOZOR**
Praha 1, Vodičkova 39, tel.: 26 36 16

**64 U HRADEB**
Praha 1, Mostecká 21, tel.: 53 50 06

## ■ ROCK CAFES AND CLUBS ■

**AKROPOLIS**
Praha 3 – Žižkov, Kubelíkova 27

**BELMONDO REVIVAL MUSIC CLUB VLTAVSKÁ**
Praha 7, Bubenečská 1

**BLATOUCH**
Praha 1, Vězeňská 4

**BORÁT ROCK CLUB** (18–06, live concerts)
Praha 1 – Malá Strana, Újezd 18, tel.: 53 83 62

**BUNKR** (10–05, live concerts)
Praha 1, Lodecká 2, tel.: 231 45 35

**DELTA CLUB**
Praha 6, Vlastina 887, tel.: 30 19 222

**FUTURUM ROCK CLUB**
Praha 5, Zborovská 7, tel.: 54 44 75

**GLOBE CAFÉ**
Praha 7, Janovského 14

**HOGO FOGO**
Praha 1 – Staré Město, Salvátorská 4

**JUNIOR CLUB**
Praha 3, Koněvova 219, tel.: 82 85 98

**KONVIKT CLUB**
Praha 1, Konviktská 22

**LEGENDA**
Praha 1, Křižovnická 12, tel.: 232 20 40

**MAMA CLUB**
Praha 1, El. Krásnohorské 7

**RADOST FX** (live concerts)
Praha 2, Bělehradská 120, tel.: 25 12 10

**REPRE CLUB** Municipal House
Praha 1, nám. Republiky 5, tel.: 24 81 10 60

**ROCK CAFÉ**
Praha 1, Národní třída 20, tel.: 24 91 44 14

**ROXY** (live concerts)
Praha 1, Dlouhá 33, tel.: 231 63 31

**STRAHOV 007**
Praha 6 – Břevnov, Spartakiádní ul.
(near Strahov Stadium)

**TAM–TAM MUSIC CLUB** Slovanský dům
Praha 1, Na Příkopě 22, tel.: 24 21 12 89

**UZI TAATOO ROCK BAR**
Praha 2, Legerova 44, tel.: 24 91 32 01

**VELRYBA** (11–02)
Praha 1, Opatovická 24

## ■ DISCO ■

**DISCOLAND SYLVIE**
Praha 8 – Libeň, Primátorská 3/172

**EDEN PALLADIUM** (21–02)
Praha 10 – Vršovice, U Slavie 1, tel.: 74 70 10

**HANAVSKÝ PAVILON**
Praha 6 – Letenské sady

**LÁVKA**
Praha 1, Novotného lávka 1, tel.: 24 21 47 97

**METRO–VAGON**
Praha 1, Národní třída 25

**MUSIC PARK**
Praha 2, Francouzská 4

**PEKLO** pasáž Světozor (20–02)
Praha 1, Vodičkova 39

**SRDÍČKO DISCO CLUB**
Praha 1, Hybernská 24

## ■ ADVANCE BOOKING OFFICES ■

**AMERICAN EXPRESS**
Praha 1, Václavské náměstí 56

**BTI**
Praha 1, Salvátorská 6, tel.: 23 22 144

**BTI**
Praha 1, Na Příkopě 16, tel.: 24 21 50 31

**BTI**
Praha 1, Václavské náměstí 25, tel.: 2422 7253

**ČEDOK**
Praha 1, Na Příkopě 18

**ČEDOK**
Praha 1, Bílkova 6

**FESTIVAL CENTRE MOZART OPEN**
Praha 1, Žatecká 1, tel.: 232 34 29

**PIS**
Praha 1, Staroměstské náměstí 22

**PIS**
Praha 1, Na Příkopě 20

**TIKETPRO – LATERNA MAGIKA**
Praha 1, Národní třída 4, tel.: 311 87 80

**TIKETPRO – LUCERNA**
Praha 1, Štěpánská 61

**TIKETPRO – MELANTRICH**
(pasáž Rokoko)
Praha 1, Václavské náměstí 38

**TIKETPRO – REDUTA**
Praha 1, Národní třída 20

**TIKETPRO PIS**
Praha 1, Staroměstské náměstí 22

**TIKETPRO**
Praha 1, Na Příkopě 20

**TOP THEATRE TICKETS**
Praha 1, Celetná 13

**VAGON LITS**
Praha 1, U Prašné brány 1

**WOLFF REISEN**
Praha 1, Na Příkopě 24

## ■ EMBASSIES AND CONSULATES ■

**AFGHANISTAN**
Praha 6, V Tišině 6, tel.: 37 24 17

**ALBANIA**
Praha 6, Pod kaštany 22, tel.: 37 93 29

**ALGERIA**
Praha 6, Na Marně 16, tel.: 24 31 11 50

**ANGOLA**
Praha 7, Nad štolou 18, tel.: 37 62 60

**ARGENTINA**
Praha 1, Washingtonova 25, tel.: 24 21 24 48

**AUSTRIA**
Praha 5, Viktora Huga 10, tel.: 24 51 16 77

**BELGIUM**
Praha 1, Valdštejnská 6, tel.: 24 51 05 32

**BOLIVIA**
Praha 2, Ve Smečkách 25, tel.: 26 32 09

**BRAZIL**
Praha 1, Bolzanova 5, tel.: 24 21 52 87

**BULGARIA**
Praha 1, Krakovská 6, tel.: 24 22 86 46

**BURMA**
Praha 6, Romaina Rollanda 3, tel.: 38 11 40

**CANADA**
Praha 6, Mickiewiczova 6, tel.: 312 02 51

**CHINA**
Praha 6, Pelléova 22, tel.: 24 31 13 23

**COLUMBIA**
Praha 1, Příčná 1, tel.: 29 13 30

**COSTARICA**
Praha 1, Dlouhá 4, tel.: 231 07 82

**CROATIA**
Praha 2, Vinohradská 69, tel.: 627 19 69

**CUBA**
Praha 6, Sibiřské nám. 1, tel.: 34 13 41

**CYPRUS**
Praha 2, Budečská 1, tel.: 25 63 76

**DENMARK**
Praha 6, U páté baterie 7, 35 31 09

**ECUADOR**
Praha 1, Opletalova 43, tel.: 236 33 22

**EGYPT**
Praha 6, Pelléova 14, tel.: 34 10 51

**ETHIOPIA**
Praha 6, V průhledu 9, tel.: 35 22 68

**FINLAND**
Praha 1, Dřevná 2, tel.: 24 91 35 94

**FRANCE**
Praha 1, Velkopřevorské nám. 2
tel.: 24 51 04 02

**GERMAN FEDERAL REPUBLIC**
Praha 1, Vlašská 19, tel.: 24 51 03 23

**GHANA**
Praha 6, V tišině 4, tel.: 37 30 58

**GREAT BRITAIN**
Praha 1, Thunovská 14, tel.: 24 51 04 39

**GREECE**
Praha 6, Na Ořechovce 19, tel.: 35 42 79

**HUNGARY**
Praha 6, Badeniho 1, tel.: 36 50 41

**INDIA**
Praha 1, Valdštejnská 6, tel.: 24 51 03 64

**INDONESIA**
Praha 1, Nad Buďánkami 11/17, tel.: 526041

**IRAN**
Praha 6, Na Zátorce 18, tel.: 37 23 73

**IRAQ**
Praha 6, Na Zátorce 10, tel.: 37 50 31

**ITALY**
Praha 1, Nerudova 20, tel.: 24 51 00 89

**ISRAEL**
Praha 7, Badeniho 2, tel.: 32 24 87

**JAPAN**
Praha 1, Maltézské nám. 6, tel.: 24 51 07 53

**KAMPUCHEA**
Praha 6, Na Hubálce 1, tel.: 35 26 03

**LATVIA**
Praha 2, Kateřinská 4, tel.: 29 89 98

**LITHUANIA**
Praha 6, Janákova 6, tel.: 311 01 94

**LEBANON**
Praha 1, Masarykovo nábř. 14, tel.: 29 36 33

**LIBYA**
Praha 6, Na baště sv. Jiří 5–7, tel.: 32 03 10

**MEXICO**
Praha 7, Nad Kazankou 8, tel.: 855 55 54

**MONGOLIA**
Praha 6, Na Marně 5, tel.: 24 31 11 98

**MOROCCO**
Praha 6, Ke starému Bubenči 4, tel.: 32 47 92

**NETHERLANDS**
Praha 1, Maltézské nám. 1, tel.: 24 51 01 88

**NICARAGUA**
Praha 7, Vinařská 1, tel.: 37 38 72

**NIGERIA**
Praha 6, Před bateriemi 18, tel.: 35 66 51

**NORWAY**
Praha 6, Na Ořechovce 69, tel.: 35 45 26

**PAKISTAN**
Praha 6, Šmolíkova 1009, tel.: 302 58 69

**PALESTINE**
Praha 6, Na Ořechovce 4, tel.: 24 31 12 65

**PERU**
Praha 3, Hradecká 18, tel.: 67 31 19 72

**POLAND**
Praha 1, Valdštejnská 8, tel.: 53 69 51

**PORTUGAL**
Praha 7, Bubenská 3, tel.: 66 71 10 65

**REPUBLIC OF COREA**
Praha 5, U Mrázovky 1985/17, tel.: 54 26 71

**RUMANIA**
Praha 1, Nerudova 5, tel.: 24 51 04 16

**SLOVAKIA**
Praha 6, Pod hradbami 1, tel.: 32 05 21

**SLOVENIA**
Praha 6, Pod hradbami 15, tel.: 34 14 31

**SOUTH AFRICA**
Praha 10, Ruská 65, tel.: 67 31 11 14

**SPAIN**
Praha 6, Pevnostní 9, tel.: 24 31 14 41

**SRI LANKA**
Praha 6, Interbrigády 3, tel.: 322 04 47

**SUDAN**
Praha 1, Malostranské nábř. 1, tel.: 53 65 47

**SWEDEN**
Praha 1, Úvoz 13, tel.: 24 51 04 36

**SWITZERLAND**
Praha 6, Pevnostní 7, tel.: 32 04 06

**SYRIA**
Praha 6, Pod kaštany 16, tel.: 24 31 11 71

**THE UNITED STATES OF AMERICA**
Praha 1, Tržiště 15, tel.: 24 51 08 47

**THE YEMEN**
Praha 1, Washingtonova 17, tel.: 22 24 11

**TUNISIA**
Praha 7, Nad kostelem 7, tel.: 24 31 11 50

**TURKEY**
Praha 6, Pevnostní 3, tel.: 24 31 14 02

**URUGUAY**
Praha 1, Václavské nám. 64, tel.: 24 21 63 77

**RUSSIA**
Praha 6, Pod kaštany 1, tel.: 38 19 40

**VATICAN**
Praha 1, Voršilská 12, tel.: 24 91 21 92

**VENEZUELA**
Praha 5, Janáčkovo nábř. 49, tel.: 2451 0767

**VIETNAMESE SOCIALIST REPUBLIC**
Praha 5, Holečkova 6, tel.: 54 64 98

**YUGOSLAVIA**
Praha 1, Mostecká 15, tel.: 53 14 43

**UNO**
Praha 1, Panská 5, tel.: 22 14 31–2

**CHILE**
Praha 6, U Vorlíků 4, tel.: 37 12 30

# ■ FOREIGN CULTURAL CENTRES ■

**AMERICAN CULTURE CENTRE**
Praha 1, Hybernská 7a, tel.: 24 23 10 85

**AUSTRIAN CULTURE INSTITUTE**
Praha 5, Victora Huga 10, tel.: 24 51 16 77

**THE BRITISH COUNCIL**
Praha 1, Národní 10, tel.: 203 751–5

**FRANCE CULTURE INSTITUTE**
Praha 1, Štěpánská 35, tel.: 24 21 66 30

**GOETHE INSTITUTE**
Praha 1, Masarykovo nábřeží 32, tel.: 24 91 57 25

**ITALIAN CULTURE INSTITUTE**
Praha 1 – Malá Strana, Sporkova 14, tel.: 2451 0204

**HUNGARIAN CULTURE CENTRE**
Praha 1, Rytířská 25–27, tel.: 24 22 24 24

**POLISH CULTURE CENTRE**
Praha 1, Václavské náměstí 19, tel.: 2421 2274

**RUSSIAN INFORMATION AND CULTURE CENTRE**
Praha 1, Rytířská 31, tel.: 22 23 56–8

**VIETNAMESE CULTURE CENTRE**
Praha 1, Havelská 29, tel. : 22 55 84

# ■ FOREIGN AIRLINES ■

**AIR FRANCE**
Praha 1, Václavské nám. 10, tel.: 24 22 71 64

**ALITALIA**
Praha 1, Revoluční 5, tel.: 2481 0079, fax: 231 4229

**AUSTRIAN AIRLINES**
Praha 1, Revoluční 15, tel.: 231 33 78, 231 18 72

**BRITISH AIRWAYS**
Praha 1, Staroměstské nám. 10, tel.: 232 90 20

**DELTA**
Praha 1, Národní 32, tel./fax: 26 71 41

**FINNAIR**
Praha 2, Španělská 2, tel.: 24 21 19 86

**KLM ROYAL DUTCH AIRLINES**
Praha 1, Václavské nám. 37, tel.: 24 22 86 78

**LOT**
Praha 1, Pařížská 18, tel.: 231 75 24

**LUFTHANSA**
Praha 1, Pařížská 28, tel.: 24 81 10 07

**SAS**
Praha 1, Štěpánská 61, tel.: 24 21 47 49

**SWISSAIR**
Praha 1, Pařížská 11, tel.: 24 81 21 11

**RUSSIAN INTERNATIONAL AIRLINES**
Praha 1, Pařížská 5, tel.: 24 81 26 83

**AIR ALGERIA**
Praha 1, Žitná 23. tel.: 24 22 91 10

**AIR INDIA**
Praha 1, Václavské nám. 15, tel.: 24 21 24 74

**AIR CANADA**
Praha 4, U Družstva Život. tel.: 643 39 34

**KUWAIT AIRWAYS**
Praha 1, Pařížská 23, tel.: 231 14 72

**MALEV HUNGARIAN AIRLINES**
Praha 1, Pařížská 5, tel.: 24 21 01 32

**TUNIS AIR**
Praha 1, Nekázanka 20, tel.: 21 24 736, 21 24 740

# ■ HOTELS ■

**AMBASSADOR **** / ZLATÁ HUSA**
Praha 1, Václavské nám. 5–7, tel.: 24 19 3111

**APOLLO GARNI ****
Praha 8, Kubišova 23, tel.: 66 41 06 28

**APOLLON ****
Praha 3, Koněvova 158, tel.: 64 42 414–7

**ARISTON ****
Praha 3, Seifertova 63, tel.: 627 98 26

**ATLANTIC ****
Praha 1 – Na Poříčí 9, tel.: 24 81 10 84

**ATOL**
Rudná u Prahy, tel.: 0311/950 701

**ATRIUM ****
Praha 8, Pobřežní 1, tel.: 24 84 11 11

**AXA ****
Praha 1, Na Poříčí 40, tel.: 24 81 25 80

**BELVEDERE ****
Praha 7, M. Horákové 19, tel.: 37 47 41

**BÍLÝ LEV ****
Praha 3, Cimburkova 20, tel.: 27 11 262

**CITY HOTEL MORÁŇ ****
Praha 2, Na Moráni 15, tel.: 24 91 52 08

**CLUB HOTEL BOHEMIA**
Praha 6, Ruzyňská 197, tel.: 31 62 401

**CLUB HOTEL PRAHA ****
Průhonice 400, tel.: 643 65 01

**COUBERTIN ****
Praha 6 – Strahov, Atletická 4, tel.: 35 28 51

**DIPLOMAT ****
Praha 6, Evropská 15, tel.: 24 39 41 11

**ESPLANADE *****
Praha 1, Washingtonova 19, tel.: 24 21 17 15

**EVROPA ***
Praha 1, Václavské nám. 25, tel.: 24 22 81 17

**FAMILY HOTEL VONDRA ***
Praha 6, Na břevnovské pláni 1975/73, tel.: 355505

**FLORENC ***
Praha 8, Křižíkova 11, tel.: 24 22 32 60

**FORUM ****
Praha 4, Kongresová 1, tel.: 61 19 11 11

**GARDEN ***
Praha 4, Vítovcova 28, tel.: 47 22 919

**GLOBUS ***
Praha 4, Gregorova 2115, tel.: 792 77 00

**GRAND HOTEL BOHEMIA**
Praha 1, U Prašné brány 1

**GOLF ***
Praha 5 – Motol, Plzeňská 215a, tel.: 52 32 51

**HARMONY ***
Praha 1, Na Poříčí 31, tel.: 232 07 20

**HOFFMEISTER ****
Praha 1–Malá Strana, Pod Bruskou 9, tel.: 2451 1015

**HOTEL ADRIA PRAHA ****
Praha 1, Václavské nám. 26, tel.: 26 17 64

**HOTEL CITY ***
Praha 2, Belgická 10 , tel./fax: 69 11 334

**HYBERNIA**
Praha 1, Hybernská 24, tel.: 24 21 04 40

**INTERCONTINENTAL *****
Praha 1, nám. Curieových, tel.: 248 81 11

**INTERNATIONAL ****
Praha 6, Koulova 15, tel.: 24 39 31 11

**JALTA *****
Praha 1, Václavské nám. 45, tel.: 242 291 33

**JULIŠ ***
Praha 1, Václavské nám. 22, tel.: 24 21 70 92

**JUNIORHOTEL **
Praha 2, Žitná 12, tel.: 24 91 57 67

**JUVENTUS ***
Praha 2, Blanická 10, tel.: 25 51 51

**KAMPA**
Praha 1, Všehrdova 16, tel.: 24 51 04 09

**KARL–INN ***
Praha 8, Šaldova 54, tel.: 24 81 17 18

**KORUNA ***
Praha 1, Opatovická 16, tel.: 24 91 31 34

**MERAN**
Praha 1, Václavské nám. 27, tel.: 24 22 84 70

**METEOR PLAZA**
Praha 1, Hybernská 6, tel.: 2422 0664

**NOVOMĚSTSKÝ HOTEL**
Praha 1, Řeznická 4, tel.: 20 68 92

**OLYMPIK ****
Praha 8 – Karlín Invalidovna 138, tel.: 661 81 111

**OPERA ***
Praha 1, Těšnov 13, tel.: 231 56 09

**PALACE *****
Praha 1, Panská 12, tel.: 24 09 31 11

**PANORAMA ****
Praha 4, Milevská 7, tel.: 61 16 11 11

**PARKHOTEL ****
Praha 7, Veletržní 20, tel.: 380 711 11

**PAŘÍŽ *****
Praha 1, U Obecního domu 1, tel.: 24 22 21 51

**PRAHA *****
Praha 6, Sušická 20, tel.: 24 34 11 11

**PRAHA PENTA / HOTEL RENAISSANCE *****
Praha 1, V Celnici, tel.: 24 81 03 96

**PRESIDENT ****
Praha 1, nám. Curieových 100, tel.: 231 48 12

**PROKOP ***
Praha 5, Pod Žvahovem 50, tel./fax: 53 48 37

**PYRAMIDA ***
Praha 6 – Břevnov, Bělohorská 24, tel.: 311 32 41

**SAVOY**
Praha 1, Keplerova 6, tel.: 53 74 50

**SPIRITKA ****
Praha 5 . Atletická 115, tel.: 53 66 58

**SPLENDID ***
Praha 7, Ovenecká 33, tel.: 37 54 51

**SPORTHOTEL OAZA ***
Praha 4, Jeremenkova 106, tel.: 692 70 90

**SVORNOST**
Praha 9, Novozámecká 284, tel.: 728 256

**U LÍPY I.**
Praha 5, Plzeňská 142. tel.: 52 29 27

**UNGELT ***
Praha 1, Štupartská 1. tel.: 24 81 13 30

**UNION ***
Praha 2, Ostrčilovo nám. 4, tel.: 692 75 06

**U PÁVA ***
Praha 1 – Malá Strana, U lužického semináře 32
tel.: 24 51 09 22, fax: 53 33 79

**U TŘÍ PŠTROSŮ ***
Praha 1, Dražického nám. 12
tel.: 24 51 07 79, fax: 24 51 07 83

**U ZLATÉ STUDNĚ**
Praha 1, Karlova 3. tel.: 22 05 93

**VANÍČEK ***
Praha 5, Na Hřebenkách 60, tel.: 35 28 90

**VILLA VOYTA ****
Praha 4, K Novému dvoru 124/54
tel.: 472 55 11, fax: 472 94 26

**VÍTKOV ***
Praha 3, Koněvova 114, tel.: 27 93 41–8,

**ZLATÁ PRAHA ***
Praha 6 – Dejvice, Na Zavadilce 8, tel.: 2431 1426